THE GATHERING STORM

THE GATHERING STORM

America Under Judgment

BRIAN NEIL PETERSON AND
CHRISTINE E. CURLEY

TFC Publishing

Contents

First Printing, 2022

We would like to dedicate this book to our five children, Maddie, Mark, Kevin, Evie, and Cassie. You are the reason we do what we do. May you come to appreciate the work of God in your lives and the role of the Spirit to enlighten you about the dangers of living in a fallen world.

Introduction

Seventy-nine days! That is how long I fasted and prayed that God would intervene after the 2020 election. Let me explain. On November 3rd I felt God leading me to fast and pray the entire day as America went to the polls to decide the next President and Congress of the United States. By the end of the first day of the election—I know that sounds strange seeing how America has historically had *one* election day, the first Tuesday of November—Donald J. Trump looked to have won his second term. He was leading in all the swing states except for Arizona, but most (perhaps with the exception of Fox News) felt that this state would quickly change as the returns in the Republican stronghold of Maricopa County came in. However, under the guise and excuse of the Covid-19 pandemic, many states had hastily passed laws and/or bureaucrats had unilaterally changed or eased voting laws in order supposedly to make voting easier. In doing so, many of the key swing states (Michigan, Pennsylvania, Wisconsin, Georgia, and Arizona) allowed for the counting of ballots, in some cases, for days after the election, a decision that would come back to haunt the Republican-led legislatures in these states. As things began to look bleaker on November 4th, I remained in a state of fasting and prayer feeling that something sinister and evil was unfolding before my eyes. As a newly naturalized citizen of the United

States, this was my first experience of voting in a presidential election, and I was excited to see American democracy at work; however, my gut feelings of foreboding and spiritual urgency would prove to be correct.

From November 5th until the inauguration on January 20, 2021, I continued to fast all my lunch meals asking God for divine intervention into what was clearly an election that had too many irregularities to be considered a valid presentation of the oft touted "will of the people" or "mandate" from "we the People." I do not say these things to try and make myself appear super spiritual—I certainly do not see myself through that lens—but rather to show that I recognized the urgency of that moment in America's history and what the repercussions of the election would mean not just for me and my wife, but for my five small children moving forward. I sensed a spiritual darkness descending over the nation as the mainstream media (hereafter MSM) closed ranks around the supposed victory of the Biden and Harris ticket while the counting continued for days after November 3rd. The MSM began to hail the election of 2020 as a great victory for democracy and "the most secure and safest election in US history." I was glued to alternative conservative and Christian media sources for the next two months in the hopes that somehow God would shine a glimmer of light in the election "darkness" and give conservative Christians hope. Many of us prayed that through some means God would intervene and reverse what was becoming increasingly apparent as time went on: Joe Biden was going to be the next president of the United States. In fact, several prophetic voices were declaring that God was going to bring Trump into his second term. I relied on these voices and alternative media sources because I knew I could not rely on the MSM. They had declared the election over and any questioning of the results was of course nothing more than conspiracy theories and insurrectionist propaganda.

As my wife and I watched and discussed the issues surrounding the numerous election challenges in the courts, which were being turned aside by judges, legislatures, secretaries of state, and governors, the reality of what had transpired on November 3rd and the days that followed settled like a dark pall over our day-to-day lives. Just for the record, whenever a judge would hear an election case on its merits allowing evidence to be heard, Trump's supporters who brought the cases, or the President himself, won 71 percent of the time.[1] But this was not happening in most of the high-profile cases like Texas' Supreme Court of the United States (hereafter SCOTUS) lawsuit against Georgia, Pennsylvania, Michigan, and Wisconsin for changing their voting laws unconstitutionally. The media simply repeated the lie that every one of the court cases had been thrown out for lack of evidence. This simply was not true. Most of the court cases were thrown out on technicalities or due to the nebulous procedural statute of "standing," as if the President of the United States did not have "standing" in an election with so many questionable shenanigans (I will return to this in a later chapter). The truth was that not one judge, justice, legislator, governor, or otherwise, wanted to get involved in these cases. They instead turned a blind eye and allowed injustice and legitimate grievances to be left unheard. It seemed like they were all in cahoots working to steal the election for the Democrat candidates wherever they could, a reality that was later verified by an exposé in *Time* magazine declaring this very thing.

With every passing day, the walls of injustice were closing in on America. It was indeed a dark time. A sense of urgency and despair began to grip me as I watched injustice and obfuscation take the place of truth and justice. Indeed, I felt I was living Isaiah 59:14 in real time: "Our courts oppose people who are righteous, and justice is nowhere to be found. Truth falls dead in the streets, and fairness has been outlawed" (NLT). I knew that something was not right in this regard. Keep in mind that injustice is a theme that the prophets and Jesus often addressed as a particularly heinous crime and blight on any nation (Isa 1:17; 10:1; 61:8; Jer 7:6; 22:3; Eccl 3:16; Micah 6:8; Hab 1:13; Zech 7:10; Mal 3:5; Luke 18:1–8 etc.).

On more than one occasion my wife noted that the days and weeks immediately following November 3rd felt to her like we were living in a combination of George Orwell's *1984* and Aldous Huxley's *Brave New World*. We watched as left-leaning Americans and "Christians" hailed the Democrat victory as something to celebrate from the rooftops. In their eyes, America had been delivered from the "totalitarian," and "Nazi-like" rule of Donald J. Trump. The mean tweets would end, and the brash nature of the President would finally be silenced and removed from the political and public square. Their children would be safe now. Our country would be restored to respectability around the world. The "strong man" would be bound and cast aside as "democracy" finally righted what was hailed a horrible nightmare. The anomaly of the 2016 election could now be put in the rearview mirror, and America could move on to normalcy and return to politics as usual. What a victory it was indeed. The four-year harangue of "Orange man bad" trumpeted by every MSM channel, political and cultural pundit, late-night comedian, and left-of-center politician and voter had finally paid dividends. America had finally been exercised of its demon: Trump would be leaving office in a few short weeks, a period that could not pass fast enough for never-Trumpers, the Democrat Left, and the MSM.

On top of all the crazy and bizarre events between November 3rd and the end of the year, the fiasco of January 6, 2021, at the capital fueled the flames of vitriol leading the Democrat Speaker of the House, Nancy Pelosi, to call for the second impeachment of the President (both within a one-year period mind you) to remove Trump from office even sooner. Waiting for the final three weeks of President Trump's presidency to end would not suffice. He had to be removed now from office for the sake of the country and to "save our democracy!" The opposition also insisted that legislation had to be passed to ensure that Trump could never hold public office ever again. The long knives were out, and the mob mentality gripped those who hated Trump. There was blood in the water, and this was their chance to drive the proverbial nail in the coffin of the political career of Donald J. Trump and to keep him from ever being a thorn in their side again.

Adding to the chaos was the fact that immediately after November 3rd many prophets of God, and some not so divinely influenced, began to prophesy that Biden would never see the inside of the White House. In fact, some went so far as to say assuredly that God had showed them that Trump would be standing on the inauguration podium come

January 20, 2021, not Joseph R. Biden. I know I was not the only Christian to tune into a number of these rising and long-standing prophetic voices speaking words of encouragement and the complete victory and vindication that was coming swiftly for Trump and his supporters. God was going to have the final say, they declared! Trump would have his second term and Christians could sit back and enjoy the show—some even told their listeners to "eat cake"—as God moved and brought it all to fruition exposing the lies of the Enemy and the Left. It was like I was living in the Old Testament era again. The prophetic word was assured, all we had to do was stand still and see the power and salvation of our God.

Again, I want to make it clear that I am not trying to belittle the prophetic voice and the prophets of God. What I am saying is that I was confused as to what God was doing or going to do. Over the months of November and December I watched as it appeared that God was about to turn the tide and reveal the injustice of the election only to see it ripped from our grasp by cowardly judges, legislators, and governors. Meanwhile the Left gloated over yet another victory as the judicial branch from SCOTUS all the way down to local justices turned a blind eye to every form of election injustice imaginable: voter intimidation, ballot stuffing, illegal immigrants voting, double voting, vote flipping, mysterious late-night ballot dumps mostly for Biden, late-night counting of ballots when no one was present, political and judicial bullying of candidates and politicians who wanted fair elections and transparent audits, phantom votes, questionable adjudication of ballots, the curing of Democrat ballots but not Republican ones, unsecured drop boxes without a chain of custody for the ballots, and the list goes on. And to make matters worse, left-leaning Christians scoffed at the prophets who were saying that God was going to intervene. They declared that God's judgment was now coming upon Trump and his supporters. God was judging Trump for his hubris and God was showing his displeasure for conservative Trump supporters for idolizing and trusting in him instead of God. Just for the record, I, like many others I know, did neither.

After the apparent finality of the inauguration of January 20, 2021, I began to feel with more certainty what had been stirring in the back of my mind since November 3rd but what I had been suppressing and hoping and praying was not true. I began to accept the reality of the very thing of which every person should shudder at the thought: God's judgment was descending in full force upon the nation of America. These feelings were there from the beginning and even long before November 3rd but like many people, I hoped that I was wrong. Now, a year after the election, I have finally come to the point where I feel I must write what God has been laying on my heart. America is under judgment! The events of November 3rd, 2020 were the harbinger of the storm that was to come. In the same way Elijah's servant saw the cloud the size of a man's hand, which served as a warning of an impending deluge (1 Kgs 18:44), the events of November 3rd to January 20, 2021, served as the precursor to what was coming upon America because of her rejection of God, God's laws, and God's appointed leaders.

In light of these things, this book is an attempt to sound the alarm for America and for Christians of all stripes. What is coming is not good; it is downright frightening. Unless God intervenes, America is doomed for destruction. All the signs are now beginning to become increasingly clear. Throughout the chapters that follow I will address several of the things I have touched on in these opening pages (e.g., politics, judicial concerns, a divided church, cultural changes). As much as possible, I will also base my conclusions and assertions in the Word of God. To be sure, there are precedents established within God's revealed Word that answer many of the very things we are dealing with today in America. History does repeat itself and God's Word is sure. I also want my reader to know that as an Old Testament professor at a Christian university, I can give a perspective that is unique from the average person. This is why I will use the Bible as the basis for my argumentation.

Finally, I want to note that in the discussion that follows, my wife, Christine, will contribute throughout and offer her insights as a wife, mother, a historian, and as a trained pastor. With three degrees of her own, she is more than qualified to offer valuable insights that I have overlooked or simply not considered. When she speaks, she will identify herself, otherwise, when first person pronouns are used, it is me, Brian, who is speaking. It is our hope that this book will offer more than our own ideas and insights but will also give a Christian couple's perspective of the issues facing America and what conservative America should expect and how they should react moving forward.

2

Forecasting the Changing Weather: Did the Prophets Get It Wrong?

Cambridge's Online Dictionary defines a forecaster as: "a person who tells you what particular conditions are expected to be like" as in an economic or weather forecaster. In the Church, we regularly view the prophetic office in a similar light only from a spiritual perspective. The OT and NT are replete with examples of the prophetic office being used to warn or "forecast" future events in the life of Israel, and later, the Church. The prophetic voice is no less important today for those of us who believe the prophetic office is still in force in the Church. The problem, however, is what do we do as a Church when the "forecasters" get it wrong, or at least appear to get it wrong? In the OT, false prophets were to be marginalized, or in worse case scenarios, executed (Deut 13:5; 18:20–22). Of course, we do not do the latter today because we are under the New Covenant and do not live in a theocracy but rather democracies. Instead, today we are told to test the prophetic words (1 John 4:1). This becomes important when viewed through the lens of what has been happening in America since the fall of 2020 and the events after the election of November 3rd. Many prophets insisted that God had showed them that Trump would be the President of the US for another term. What should be the Church's response when the prophets get something so wrong?

As noted in my Introduction, one of the more disturbing trends since the November election has been the confusion surrounding God's use, or non-use, of the prophetic office. While some prophesied that Trump would not be removed from office, others insisted that God was judging conservative evangelicals for their "blind" and idolatrous "worship" of President Trump. As the days and weeks ticked by after the election, it became increasingly clear that those prophesying a consecutive second term for Trump were in fact wrong, or at least it was appearing that way. Some began to backtrack about their prophecies and offer public apologies on social media for what they had declared to be the unquestionable truth of God's revealed word to them. It made the prophetic office appear as a mockery to the world and those who have rejected the notion of God moving in such a manner. At the same time, other prophets and prophetesses continued to insist that they were not wrong. Some simply noted, albeit perhaps correctly, that Trump had won the election but that it had been stolen from him. In light of this theft, they insisted, and some continue to insist, that Trump would/will in fact have a second term with God removing Biden from office in the near future and restoring Trump to office. As of mid-2021, there were a number of prophets saying this very thing. And as of the first half of 2022, some prophets have come to the conclusion that God must act quickly or they will be viewed as false prophets. So, who is right?

Before answering this question, I want to offer a couple of caveats about what I am going to be dealing with below. First, I will not name specific prophets and prophetesses when I speak about this difficult topic. To do so would give the appearance that I am heaping shame and derision on people who may already be feeling despondent because of what they have spoken in God's name that did not come to fruition. Second, as you read through this chapter, I pray that you will recognize that I am not trying to diminish or apologize for the prophetic office, but rather I am trying to explain why or how the prophetic voice seemed to get it so wrong. Finally, I am convinced that unless God intervenes, America is indeed on the path of God's judgment. The prophetic voice in this regard is accurate if biblical history is any indication of how God acts.

Scriptural Precedents of Apparent Failure of the Prophetic Voice

Scripturally, is there a precedent for such contradictory or competing voices among the prophets? There are several biblical examples of competing prophetic voices, some of which contrast false prophets with the true prophets of God. Two of the more prominent examples of prophetic confrontation are those of Jeremiah and Hananiah in Jeremiah 28 (cf. Jer 6:13–15) and the conflict between Micaiah and the false prophets of Ahab in 1 Kings 22. In both cases, the text makes it clear that the false prophets were at odds with the true prophets because they were speaking from their own desires and imaginations. Put differently, they were speaking what *they* wanted to see come to pass as opposed to what God had actually told them. A fine example of this appears in the life of Nathan the prophet. Nathan's assertion that God was with David when he desired to build the temple demonstrates that sometimes even the most ardent and devout prophet may misunderstand God's true will. Nathan had to come back later and tell David he was wrong (2 Sam 7:3–7). Nathan appears to have spoken what *he* wanted to see as opposed to what God wanted. There can be little doubt that this was a factor in what happened after the 2020 election. Many people spoke what *they* had desired for an outcome. In this category, it is probably safe to conclude that there were many who were not speaking for God.

On the other hand, what are we to do with those prophetic voices who had a track record of "getting it right" in the past? There were several in this camp. Did they get it wrong when they said God was going to intervene? I want to handle this group in two different ways. First, there are those who may have misunderstood what they were seeing in the spiritual realm. That is, they may have assumed something they were seeing was for the immediate future when in fact it was still for a future date. Second, there may have been some who did see the reality of what God wanted to do between November 3rd and January 20, 2021, but God relented for some reason. Perhaps God even changed His mind because of the actions of His people.

In the first instance, the prophetic perspective is often misunderstood even by those of the biblical period. Some have suggested that biblical characters like Paul and the disciples may have misunderstood the timing of Jesus' return, thinking it would be in their lifetime (cf. John 21:22–23; 1 Cor 15:51–58; 1 Thess 4) when in fact the age of the Gentiles (Rom 9–11) would be a much longer period than anticipated. This has been also argued for Ezekiel's prophetic words about Tyre and Sidon in Ezekiel 26. Did he get it wrong when Nebuchadnezzar did not complete the destruction of the island portion of the nation of Tyre? It seems more likely that Ezekiel saw the destruction of the island fortress in the period of Alexander the Great. What the prophets, both ancient and modern, sometimes do is conflate two events which will happen over an expanse of time and not consecutively.

Another way misunderstandings can happen is in the *interpretations* of a prophet's words. For example, modern Jewish people reject Jesus as Messiah because when he came to the earth in the first century, he did not fulfill the prophecies of Isaiah that the Messiah would establish his kingdom and that the lion would lay down with the lamb during his reign (Isa 11:6; 65:25; cf. Acts 1:6). Again, modern Jewish interpreters conflate Jesus' first and second comings. The first coming of Jesus was his moment to be the Suffering Servant (see Isa 53, 61); however, his second return will be marked by his earthly kingship and harmony in nature as predicted by Isaiah. The prophet was not wrong, it has been Jewish *interpretation* of the prophet's words which has been wrong.

Applying this to the prophetic words during the election cycle could help explain some of the apparent discrepancies. Have the prophets missed a gap of time that will transpire between Trump's two terms? Is there still a possibility that these prophecies will come to pass in God's timing? Based upon the scriptural precedent I would have to argue in the affirmative. Indeed, this could still happen although it would have to be soon because of Trump's actual physical age. He is not getting any younger so God would have to move quickly. Either way, I am fully convinced that God could act quickly and decisively if He so desired. My concern is that we may be placing too much weight on the spiritual capital that America has with God. Time and again, in the midst of injustice, God has not acted but rather allowed a nation to go through judgment because of the buildup of sin. God's judgment on Israel and Judah are two cases in point because they had come to the point of judgment even though there were righteous people present (cf. Ezek 14:14–20; 21:1–4). Is God now allowing America to reap the whirlwind because of the seeds of injustice, paganism, depravity, and outright rejection of His divine mandates? It is certainly possible.

Did God Change His Mind?

The second argument is that God could change His mind concerning a prophetic word or people can do things to thwart the actual plan of God. I know this will ruffle a few feathers of my Reformed friends but let me explain what I mean from a biblical perspective. The clearest example of God changing His mind about doing something prophesied by His prophet can be found in the book of Jonah. Jonah prophesied the judgment of Nineveh only to have God reverse His decision when the people repented (Jonah 3–4). Was Jonah a false prophet? No, he actually delivered God's word, but God changed His mind because of the actions of the Ninevites.

Similarly, there is also an example from the book of Jeremiah which shows that God can change what has been decreed for a nation if the people do something to cause God to make the change. In Jeremiah 18:7–10 God makes it clear that if He has declared judgment on a nation (no doubt through the prophetic word) and a nation turns from their evil, then God will relent and allow the nation to live. This is exemplified in the book of Jonah. Conversely, if God has declared good for a nation and they turn and do evil, then He will change His plans and bring judgment upon that nation. This is a clear example of what happened to Judah and Israel. Even though they were the people of the covenant and God had promised them blessings (Deut 28:1–15), God sent them into exile because of their sin.

Now, applying this to the period in which we are currently living, a couple things could be in play. First, God may have desired for Trump to have a second term consecutively, but the Church refused to back him (see Chapter 4 below). Because of the lack of unity from the Church and a lack of proper support, God has allowed judgment to come upon America sooner rather than later (see more in Chapter 3 below). There is little doubt that many self-professing Christians opted to either vote for Biden and Harris or chose not to vote at all. In this case, God's people thwarted the plan of God and nullified what the prophets have seen and openly declared.

Again, there are biblical examples of people thwarting the plans of God spoken through the prophets. When Huldah the prophetess prophesied that Josiah would die in peace (2 Kgs 22:20) did she get it wrong when Josiah actually died in a war setting, not in peace? Now to be sure, there are a variety of ways Huldah's words can be interpreted. It is true that Josiah did not see the judgment of Judah spoken of by the prophets. He died before Judah went into exile, thus allowing him technically to "die in peace." But this is not the only way to view these events. In reality, Josiah went against God's plan by attacking Pharaoh Necho even though the Pharaoh warned Josiah not to engage him in battle lest God destroy him for interfering. The Chronicler notes this very thing (2 Chron 35:20–23). In case some may be thinking this is too vague, I would also note the reign of Saul. Samuel notes that Saul's dynasty/kingdom would have endured forever had he not sinned by usurping the prerogative of the prophet in sacrificing to God (1 Sam 13:13; cf. 1 Sam 15:11).

Based upon these few examples, there is clear biblical precedent showing that God changes His mind in some cases and does not fulfill the word of the prophets. Ironically, when the word of the prophet declares that God is going to do good for a people or nation and God rescinds that word, judgment is what ensues. This is what I am feeling is the case facing America. This brings me to my next point.

What Does the Proliferation of the Prophetic Voice Tell Us?

I want to end this portion of my chapter by sounding a warning about those who diminish or downplay the prophetic voice and the office. The gift of prophecy is still vitally important today (1 Cor 12:28; 14:3, 29–32; Eph 2:20; 3:5; 4:11 etc.). From a scriptural perspective, it is self-evident that once God has decreed judgment is coming, God will give ample warning through the voice of the prophets (Amos 3:7). This played itself out before the coming of judgment upon the nation of Israel and Judah. In both cases, God grouped prophets together to warn of coming judgment. Prior to the destruction and exile of the Northern Kingdom of Israel in 722 BC by the Assyrians, God sent Hosea and Amos over two decades before this event to warn of coming judgment. God also sent Micah and Isaiah at the same time to give Judah ample warning that they could suffer the same fate. Later, prior to the three exiles and ultimate destruction of Judah and Jerusalem at the hand of Babylon (ca. 604, 597, 586 BC), God sent Zephaniah, Habakkuk, Obadiah, Jeremiah, and even Ezekiel to warn of coming judgment. The people rejected the words of the prophets in every case.

Today I feel we are seeing an increase in the prophetic office for this very reason. Again, there are some conflicting prophecies regarding God's plan for the future of America. Some are saying that God is going to send a great move of the Spirit and a revival (see more in Chapter 12); that God will restore America to its origins rooted in a Judeo-Christian ideal. I would answer to this with, may it be so! This in fact may happen, but I am not overly optimistic based upon the trajectory of the nation and its consistent downward spiral into the abyss of sexual and cultural chaos. These types of happenings are hallmarks of a nation under judgment. The OT is replete with a similar pattern, especially during the judges' period and the era of the classical writing prophets (ca. 8th century to the 6th century BC). That is not to say that God cannot do a quick work before this happens. This seems to be a strong possibility based upon many trusted prophetic voices. I am simply not convinced that America will be pulled from the brink. I say this more as a historian, not a prophet. I do not identify as the latter.

With this in mind, I have come to the conclusion that God is warning us of coming judgment unless we get our lives and country in line with God's plan. While I will be dealing with this topic in more detail in a later chapter, suffice it to say that the prophets have been sounding the warnings that God is displeased with the direction of America and of the Church. I am thinking of the poignant words of David Wilkerson from the 1970s and 1980s in particular. His book published in 1985 titled *Set the Trumpet to Thy Mouth* was disturbing in this regard. We need to act with more than lip service, we need to have a heart change. This latter concept exemplified the period of Josiah as well as the time following his death. The people of Judah followed his lead to "return" to God and to accept Josiah's spiritual reforms as long as he was alive. However, after Josiah's death in 609 BC, the nation quickly walked away from God, proving that they truly did not have a heart change. In the short span of time from 609 BC until the destruction and exile of Jerusalem and Judah in 586 BC, Judah had four different kings whose rules alternated between three months and eleven years (Jehoahaz—3 month; Jehoiakim—11 years; Jehoiachin—3 months; Zedekiah—11 years). It was clear that the people had performed lip service only and as such quickly reaped God's judgment. We need to be committed to God and His plan for His Church, and for America.

Finally, I want to end this chapter by noting that just because some of the prophetic words have not come to pass as expected does not mean that all the prophets were wrong. On the contrary, as I noted above some prophets are still insisting that the word of the prophets concerning God's intervention in the 2020 election and in American politics in general is not failing but that they will come to pass in God's timing. To be sure, this very thing happened in the period of Ezekiel when the prophetic word appeared to be lapsing and languishing. At the end of the day, God did fulfill His word to bring about judgment and to vindicate His prophets (cf. Ezek 12:21–28). That said, it is still possible that God will intervene if God's people will humble themselves and pray and turn from their wicked ways (2 Chron 7:14).

I would like to offer one prophetic word as an example of this possible switch in the fortunes of America. This word was delivered by a prophet named Kim Clement several years ago in 2008 before the chaos of the 2020 election cycle. Clement, who passed away in 2016, declared that in the coming days they (the American people) would say, how can there be two presidents! He went on to note that there would be a time of exposing corruption but that this was needed before moving into the next election, and onward into a period marked by victory, honor, and glory.[2] Are we seeing this playing out before our eyes now as one half of America believes Trump is the duly elected president and Biden is illegitimate? Will the audits expose the corruption of the Left in time to have fair elections moving forward in 2022 and 2024? Other prophets have insisted that Trump will only be restored to power if Christians pray hard to get him across the proverbial finish line. I will admit that I have never seen or heard so many Christians praying for God to intervene as I have since November 3rd. If God is going to act, He certainly can choose to do so. This is especially true if Donald Trump is God's chosen man for the office of the presidency. This is the topic of my next chapter.

3

❦

The Devastating Nor'easter: Is Trump a Cyrus or Josiah Figure?

Weather.com defines a nor'easter as "a strong area of low pressure along the East Coast of the United States that typically features winds from the northeast off the Atlantic Ocean – hence the term 'nor'easter.'"[3] There can be little doubt that Donald J. Trump's meteoric rise to power in the Republican Party and his ultimate winning of the White House took everyone by surprise. Trump devastated the political class and upset the proverbial apple cart. In this regard, one could easily make the comparison between the chaos and devastation of a true nor'easter storm and Trump, a billionaire businessman from the Northeast of America, who left political devastation in his path as he challenged the status quo from 2016–2021.

After the election of Donald J. Trump in 2016, many left-leaning Christians tried to figure out how an outsider like Trump ended up being elected by a vast majority (81%) of evangelicals. What was it about Trump that appealed to Christian evangelical voters? On the one side, the Left was beside themselves trying to figure out why so-called

Christians voted for such an immoral man. David Horowitz captures the tension well when he writes, "The left could not fathom why Christians preferred a morally flawed man, in Trump, who promised to defend religious liberty over a morally flawed woman, in Hillary, who was bound to take it away."[4] On the other side, the Christian Right, especially conservative evangelicals, saw in Trump a "savior" of sorts. As such, it did not take long before biblical parallels began to be offered in an effort to explain this quandary. One of the more popular parallels was the Trump=Cyrus connection. Conversely, the elite and mainline "Christians" insisted that Trump was an abomination to the entire idea of what a president of the US should be (see more in my next chapter). In fact, many insisted that conservative evangelicals had sold their proverbial soul to the devil in voting for such a lewd and base individual like Donald Trump. For the next four years between 2016 and the election of 2020 left-leaning evangelicals (just for the record I think that pairing is an oxymoron) published a plethora of books denouncing both conservative evangelicals and the President as being a blight on what it means to be "Christian" and a civil and decent human being. Having read several of these books myself, I was taken aback at how vitriolic these authors were especially to their fellow Christians.

As I have asked many times, who is correct in their assessment of Donald J. Trump? Conservative evangelicals or their counterparts? Indeed, whom should we trust? Conservative evangelicals or the elite evangelicals in the publishing field and those who present regularly at the leading biblical studies organizations? In this chapter I want to examine the parallels between Trump and Cyrus and offer an alternate understanding of Trump's presidency in light of my ongoing thesis that America is under judgment. I will also try to offer responses to the questions I have just posited above as well as other questions that perhaps you, the reader, may be thinking. This discussion will also naturally lead to the problem of what it means for left-leaning evangelicals and mainstream church adherents to reject the presidency of Trump if in fact he was/is God's appointed leader. I will delve into this latter issue in more detail in my next chapter.

Trump and Cyrus Paralleled

Lance Wallnau offers one of the more sustained treatments of the Trump=Cyrus parallel in two of his more recent books. The first was published just prior to Trump's election in 2016, and the other came out just before the 2020 election.[5] For those who have never read these books, or if you are unfamiliar with who this Cyrus figure is, I will begin by giving a brief overview of who Cyrus was and what the Bible has to say about him.

Cyrus the Great was a Persian ruler who conquered the then-known world and ruled from 559 BC until his death in 530 BC. The Persian Empire survived until it was overthrown by the Greek ruler, Alexander the Great in 331 BC. Cyrus conquered Babylon in October of 539 BC thus becoming the ruler of the ancient Near East having now gained control of the Neo-Babylonian Empire. The events of Daniel 5 tell of the very night when Belshazzar, the son of the Babylonian ruler Nabonidus, lost his life at the hands of the Persians, and Persia took control of the city of Babylon. Daniel explains that this was due to Belshazzar's inappropriate use of the temple vessels (Dan 5:23).

Isaiah the prophet (ca. 740–680 BC) speaks of Cyrus in glowing terms (cf. Isa 41:2–4, 25; 44:28; 45:1–6; 46:11). In 44:28a he says, "*It is I who says of Cyrus, 'He is My shepherd! And he will perform all My desire'*" (NASB). Also in 45:1–6 Isaiah prophesies,

> Thus says the LORD to Cyrus His anointed, Whom I have taken by the right hand, To subdue nations before him, And to loose the loins of kings; To open doors before him so that gates will not be shut: This is what the LORD says: 'I will go before you, Cyrus, and level the mountains. I will smash down gates of bronze and cut through bars of iron. And I will give you the treasures of darkness, And hidden wealth of secret places, In order that you may know that it is I, The LORD, the God of Israel, who calls you by your name. For the sake of Jacob My

servant, And Israel My chosen *one*, I have also called you by your name; I have given you a title of honor Though you have not known Me. I am the LORD, and there is no other; Besides Me there is no God. I will gird you, though you have not known Me; That men may know from the rising to the setting of the sun That there is no one besides Me. I am the LORD, and there is no other' (NASB).

I cited Isaiah at length for the purpose of showing some of the more striking parallels between Cyrus and Trump. God chose Cyrus for a purpose, namely, to help the people of Israel and to do the will of God in this regard. God also called Cyrus "my shepherd" and God's "anointed." God even says that He has called Cyrus by his name (45:4). Isaiah makes it clear that it is God who will give Cyrus the power to do the things that he accomplishes. Surprisingly though, God recognizes that Cyrus has not known the God of Israel (45:4, 5). To be sure, Cyrus was not a "Christian" or a "God-fearer," he was a pagan used by God for the purpose of freeing the people of Israel. This freedom came when Cyrus issued his degree in 539 BC that the Jews could return to their land and rebuild their temple to Yahweh. The prophetic word of Isaiah delivered roughly 200 years before the reign of Cyrus has been challenged by scholars. Many insist that God did not give Isaiah the specific name of Cyrus 200 years in advance. Instead, they propose that this was added later after Cyrus came to power. This scholarly debate is beyond the scope of what I am covering here but I do want you, my reader, to know how many elite evangelicals interpret these texts.

Having noted these scriptural references to Cyrus, I now want to look at how Trump parallels this sixth-century Persian leader. First, although Trump may have connections to the Christian faith through his parents, I cannot speak definitively whether he is a follower of Jesus. That is between him and his Maker. Based upon many of his actions I would argue that he does not display the fruits of the Spirit, at least when he came into office. Nevertheless, one does not need to have a "Christian" president in order for God to use him or her. In the case of

Cyrus, he was a pagan, yet God used him. I think this is what God did with Donald Trump. Now that is not to say that God cannot save him, or that God is not working in his life, but rather that when he came into office the evidence of his Christian faith was minimal at best. That said, when elite evangelicals mock their conservative counterparts for not supporting a God-fearing or "respectable" president my immediate response is; whom do you suggest? Barack Obama? Hillary Clinton? Joe Biden? Kamala Harris? These four are the epitome of paganism with their support for abortion and radical social and sexual agendas (more on this in a later chapter).

Second, it is God who called Cyrus by name, not the people. Interestingly, back in 2007 the prophet Kim Clement named Trump specifically as being chosen by God to lead this nation.[6] And in the same year Clement noted that this leader that God chooses would have two terms.[7] I want to begin by saying that I believe in the divine inspiration of Scripture and the ability of the Spirit to reveal to the prophets specific information and, yes, even names of those who will rule in the future (see 1 Kgs 13:2). After all, that is what a prophet is supposed to be able to do, is it not? When Trump came into office, this prophetic word by Clement was hailed by many prophets as proof that God was behind the upset victory of Donald J. Trump in 2016. The issue that remains is the prophecy concerning the second term for Trump. While I addressed this in my previous chapter, I do want to point out that Clement did not, to my knowledge, say they would be consecutive terms. Having listened to his prophecy, he does not make this claim. Nevertheless, even if this was his intent, my arguments from my previous chapter concerning God's ability to change historical events at His behest apply here as well.

Third, God gave Cyrus the strength to do the many feats of conquest as well as the ability and insight to enact many positive policy decisions. These acts made Cyrus a great leader. It goes without saying that God gave Trump wisdom to lead America into a time of unprecedented prosperity if one is to go by the Dow Jones Industrial Average, the low unemployment numbers, and the barometer of rising wages. Until the

Covid-19 pandemic, Trump was on track to have one of the most successful presidencies in the history of America in relation to economic gains. Historic low unemployment rates for African Americans, Hispanics, and women are just three indicators. Trump also had successes in Israeli-Arab peace agreements. During his first term he brokered the signing of four treaties between Israel and her former hostile neighbors: Bahrain, the United Arab Emirates, Sudan, and Morocco. Trump also had success in the areas of NATO negotiations, the ending of the ISIS threat, the renegotiations of NAFTA, and his response to Covid-19 with Operation Warp Speed. These are just a few of the many accomplishments for which the MSM never wanted to give the President credit.

Finally, God used Cyrus to bless the people of Israel. God stirred up Cyrus to allow the Jewish people to return to their land and to rebuild their temple in Jerusalem (Ezra 4–6). One of the more disconcerting false accusations against President Trump was the claim that he was like Hitler or that he fostered white supremacy or Nazism with his patriotic "America-first" policy. This nationalistic fervor, according to his opponents, was equal to the rise of Nazism in Germany in the 1930s. Of course, this was nothing more than the propaganda of the Left, who are truly the fascists in our midst. In reality, Trump did more for the state of Israel than any of the presidents of our recent history. He is not an anti-Semite. After all, his own son-in-law is of Jewish descent! Apart from the numerous peace accords, Trump also kept his election promise to move the US embassy from Tel Aviv to Jerusalem. Israel had no better friend than Donald Trump and the Arab countries knew it. For this reason, and the fact that Trump was a no-nonsense type of guy, many feel that the Middle East calmed down under his presidency because our enemies knew Trump would enforce any warnings he sent. Not surprisingly, this is another parallel between Trump and Cyrus. God gave Cyrus the ability to "loosen the loins" of kings (Isa 45:1). One interpretation of this phrase is that Cyrus' presence not only caused kings to have their sword and war belt removed from their loins through conquest, but it may also mean that Cyrus' mere presence and manner caused people to have loose bowels for fear. In vernacular terms, this would be like us saying that they "crapped" themselves with fear. Today the Israeli-Palestinian conflict is ablaze once again under the weak foreign policy of Biden and due to Biden's affinity for Palestinian causes. This is no less true of the fiasco of the Afghan withdrawal and the complete takeover of Afghanistan by the Taliban, who were once on the run from the US. Currently, we are witnessing the aggression of Russia against the Ukraine. Biden's feckless policies are diametrically opposite to that of Trump's.

Based upon this brief overview, it is clear why many prophets and believers have come to the conclusion that Trump was a lot like Cyrus. If this is the case, then it seems very likely that God did in fact put him into power. I will address what this means for those Christians who opposed him in my next chapter. While all these parallels point to God's intervention in American politics for the purpose of bringing America into a time of greatness once again, and to aid in the peace of Israel, what happens when we the People allow a God-ordained President to be removed from office, either through a "democratic" vote or through election fraud? Does this mean that God has removed His favor from us and is bringing judgment upon us? Barring God's miraculous intervention, I think that this is in fact where America is heading and there is a solid biblical parallel for it. That is in the life of Josiah.

Trump Paralleled to Josiah

To my knowledge, no one has ever drawn a parallel between Trump and King Josiah. Josiah was the last God-fearing king of Judah who ruled from 640 BC until his death in 609 BC at the hands of Pharaoh Necho. What was unique about Josiah was that he brought about economic success in his nation, an expansion of the influence of Judah in the region, and a spiritual revival in the land. Put simply, Josiah oversaw a return to the God-focused policies of the past. He was truly the first MAGA candidate. Prior to Josiah's reign, however, Judah had done great wickedness in the eyes of God and God had declared that judgment was going to come upon the nation of Judah because of the shedding of innocent blood by Josiah's grandfather, Manasseh (2 Kgs 21:16; 24:4; cf. Jer 19:4; 22:3, 17 etc.). Yet, God delayed the judgment he promised upon Judah because of the policies and God-fearing nature of Josiah. It was not until his untimely death at the Battle of Megiddo in 609 BC, that God set in motion the rapid decline and exile of Judah at the hands of the Babylonians in 586 BC. In a little over twenty years, Judah was no more.

Where this comes into play in the life of America is in how one views the role of Trump in delaying God's judgment on America. Make no mistake, God will judge America for its paganism and ungodly laws and culture, not the least of which is the blight and abomination of abortion. Since the *Roe v. Wade* decision of 1973, America has aborted over 63 million babies. This is the shedding of innocent blood to a degree unheard of in American history. And now, it has been reported that the University of Pittsburgh is responsible for keeping "fetal organs" that were harvested while babies were still alive, babies from 6 weeks to 42 weeks![8] Think about that. These are full term babies and beyond. Under Barack Obama's presidency, abortion was hailed as a blessing and sexual proclivities of all types were praised and sanctioned by law (e.g., the 2015 *Obergefell v. Hodges* SCOTUS decision). I remember at the time of the legalization of gay marriage and Obama lighting up the White House in rainbow lights thinking that America was crossing a line from which it may never recover unless God intervened. The praising of abortion, which is nothing more than the shedding of innocent blood, causes the Manasseh=Obama parallel to have merit. When Trump won the 2016 election I felt as though God was giving America a reprieve. This reprieve I had hoped would last for several election cycles. Unfortunately, this was not to be the case.

Now again, I am not saying that Trump is Josiah. On the contrary, what I am saying is that history repeats itself and the biblical accounts serve as examples for us to learn from and as warnings. Paul notes this well in his letter to the Corinthian believers (1 Cor 10:11). When we removed God's appointed leader from office prematurely, much like Josiah died prematurely, then I believe that this paved the way for

God's judgment on America. Again, there is biblical precedent for such actions. When the children of Israel rejected God's choice of Moses as leader God judged them (Num 12, 14, 16). And when Israel sided with Absalom against God's anointed King David, God judged them again (2 Sam 24:1, 11–25). That is why I feel that the chaos which is unfolding in our country is the beginning of that judgment: gas shortages after having an excess, BLM riots, Antifa thugs roaming the streets, anti-Semitism on the rise, inflation taking off after years of being close to zero, socialism and Marxism taking center stage, critical race theory (hereafter CRT) being used to brainwash our children and military, border anarchy, draconian vaccine mandates, threats of job loss, FBI intimidation, government overreach of all kinds, illegal legislation threatening the freedom of Christian institutions, the usurping of the Constitutional rights of states, and the list goes on (see Chapter 5). While I will delve into this topic in more detail below, what I will note here is that something is stirring in America, and it is not godly. It is the flames of anarchy being fanned by the Left.

Other Possible Harbingers of Coming Judgment

Before leaving this topic there are a couple of other interesting biblical parallels I see between what happened to Donald Trump and with what is currently going on in America. I see connections between how the religious elite treated Jesus and how the religious elite treated Trump. I also see eschatological parallels between Paul's teaching on the end times and what we are experiencing today. It seems redundant, but I must preface this section once again with the caveat that I am not likening Trump to Jesus nor am I likening him to the Church. What I want my reader to notice are the historical and theological parallels between the following two examples.

First, I find it telling that when Jesus walked the earth it was the religious and political elite who caused him the most grief. He did not have trouble with the publicans and sinners (that is the "deplorables") but rather Jesus ran afoul of the political crowd and what it meant to be Roman or at least a "respectable" Jew under Roman occupation. It is not a far stretch to note that Trump ran afoul of the political elite because he did not do things their way. He was not part of the "establishment;" he came to challenge it. Moreover, Jesus had a constant struggle with the religious elite because he was not "kosher" and "couth." In their eyes, Jesus was a wine-drinking, carousing, irreverent, and lawbreaking rabble rouser. The fact that Jesus was not like they were finds interesting parallels with how the religious elite among the evangelical crowd in particular viewed Trump's candidacy and then his presidency and reelection bid. When God sent Trump to help support the unborn, the Church, and the Judeo-Christian ideals of our country, the religious elite spent their time attacking him. I have heard more than one commentator make this connection and I cannot help but agree with their assessment. Without a doubt, Trump ruffled feathers among many, especially those who saw themselves as exhibiting the "right" manner of how to be "godly." Again, the truth is, Trump was more friendly to Christians than any other president in living memory. He hosted prayer breakfasts, attended and spoke at the 2018 March for Life (the first sitting president to do so), and he invited evangelical leaders to the White House to voice their concerns about policy decisions. Despite these positive qualities, all the religious elite could see is his brash behavior and his harsh tweets. In the end, the religious elite of the first century crucified Jesus. And in the end, the religious elite of the twenty-first century praised Trump's two impeachment trials and "crucified" him weekly in their sermons, on their daily blogs, and in their multiple publications.

Second, while I will cover the issues of lawlessness and chaos in more detail in Chapter 5, I feel it necessary to at least point out a few important points at this juncture of my discussion. Since the inauguration of Biden, pandemonium has begun to sweep across our country both politically and economically. Turmoil is also sweeping through the Middle East and now Europe. It is also important to note that the lawlessness of the Executive branch and the Congress is daily reaching new heights as the MSM praises everything the Democrats do and propose, no matter how detrimental to our country. Good examples are the Democrats' desire to usurp states' rights on election law (HR1) and cultural issues (HR5), and their desire to destroy America financially by spending us into oblivion with numerous multi-trillion-dollar spending bills using the congressional loophole of "Reconciliation" so they do not have to have bi-partisan support. Since the fiasco of November 3, 2020, the Left has become emboldened to exercise racist propaganda and oppression like never before. The fact that the border is out of control is another example of the lawlessness. Make no mistake, on this latter issue, this is the Democrats' way of replacing you, the American citizen, in the voting booth with illegals, which will allow the Democrats to be in power perpetually. In one month in the fall of 2021, over 200,000 illegals entered the US on the southern border! This is the equivalent of replacing my home county of Bradley, TN, one of the most conservative counties in TN, twice in just one month! Conversely, while Trump was president he fought against cultural and racial oppression at the hands of big government. He also tried to unite the nation under the banner of American patriotism and our shared history and traditions, both Christian and secular. Trump secured our borders and reinstituted law and order. Trump was also committed to seating conservative Constitutionalists on the Supreme Court, something that has decades-long repercussions. In many ways, conservative evangelicals viewed Trump's presidency as a bulwark against the extremes of the Left.[9] This brings me to my next point.

I see an interesting parallel between the role of Trump as a "restrainer" of the corrupt Left and the teaching of Paul about the one who restrains evil.[10] In 2 Thessalonians 2:5–8 Paul says, "Do you not remember that while I was still with you, I was telling you these things? And you know what restrains him now, so that in his time he may be revealed. For the mystery of lawlessness is already at work; only he who now restrains *will do so* until he is taken out of the way. And then that lawless one will be revealed whom the Lord will slay with the breath of His mouth and bring to an end by the appearance of His coming" (NASB). Many believers have assumed that this restrainer whom Paul is talking about is the Church or perhaps the Holy Spirit (I disagree with the latter assertion). When God removes the Church, perhaps in a rapture, then all hell will break loose in the world. This is no doubt true in part; however, the reality is we are seeing this happen in our current situation in America since the Left has seized power. From a political perspective, some have argued that the downfall of America and its positive influence on the world could also be seen as a restrainer.[11] For me, I think it is possible that President Trump acted as a restrainer of sorts. While I would never liken Trump to the Church, he did, nonetheless, withhold the onslaught of the Left and its radicalism. Since January 20, 2021, we are being overrun with wickedness like we have not seen in generations, perhaps ever in America. We are seeing first-hand what happens when a person as strong as Trump is removed; evil and chaos is unleashed and grips our nation and ripples out to other nations. In reality this is a battle that is not so much political as it is spiritual. What we are witnessing today is a marriage of the Left and the demonic. We are seeing it play out in the halls of Congress, in the back rooms of the Deep State, in our K–12 classrooms and in our universities. Paul was correct: when godly influences are removed, then evil will proliferate. I feel judgment is now beginning because we have thrown off the leadership God has sent for such a time as this.

Conclusion

God's provision of a man to help lead our nation at a difficult time and God's mercy to give the Church an ally in the White House should not be downplayed especially in light of the chaos we are experiencing under this current administration. If the radical Democrats are allowed to pass HR1, either now or in a future congress, a conservative will never occupy the White House again. The corruption of the California recall election of September 2021 is a clear example of this reality. Upon surviving his recall election through the corrupted mail-in voting scheme of the Left, Governor Newsome immediately made universal mail-in voting the law of California, a system that has been proven time and again to be rife with corruption and favor the Left. This corrupt governor codified into law the Left's theft of all future elections. If we allow this type of legislation at the national level, there can be no question that this will be one more example of how God has given America over to its own devices because we have not stood up and fought against the evil of the Left and the agenda of the Socialists and Marxists. As I just noted, my personal belief is that because we have rejected God's appointed leader, we are now experiencing the judgment of God. Some of the responsibility for this current and coming judgment must be placed at the feet of so-called "liberal" Christians who hated Trump more than they loved righteousness and what was best for our country.

4

⧉

The Darkening Clouds: The Spiritual Blindness of Liberal Christianity

Darkening clouds can tell us two things. First, they can warn us that a storm is brewing and that we must seek shelter. Second, they can block out the sun and cast dark shadows across the land making it hard to see things clearly, especially if you are in a building with few windows. In a way, both these phenomena apply to what is happening in the American Church and within evangelicalism. The primary reason that spiritual darkness is descending across America is due to the spiritual blindness of liberal Christianity even though they assert that they are seeing life and politics "clearly." What is more, they are publishing and presenting unbiblical and left-of-center material which is bringing spiritual blindness and darkness to those who imbibe from their drivel. This naturally perpetuates the spiritual blindness and the spiritual darkness of self-professing "liberal Christians." In many ways this spiritual darkness can be represented by the metaphorical darkening clouds accompanying the storm of God's judgment on America. Allow me to explain.

My earliest memories of getting politically involved was struggling with the reality that a large number of so-called "Believers" voted "liberal" consistently in elections in my home country of Canada. I often wondered how this was possible in light of the wicked policies of the Left (e.g., abortion and a troubling sexual ethic). Since those early days in the 1980s, the Left's push to enact even more atrocious and ungodly policies has only increased across all ten provinces and three territories of the country of my birth. When I moved to Tennessee in 2011 to take up a teaching post at a Christian university, I was glad to be moving to the so-called "buckle of the Bible belt" of the United States. The city where I moved was also the headquarters for the Church of God. I figured the vast majority of Christians would be more conservative in their politics. What I found was a situation almost as troubling as what I experienced in my home province of New Brunswick, Canada. While there certainly were more Christian conservatives who voted their biblical values in my new home, I still could see that many self-professing Christians lined up on a regular basis to "pull the lever" for politicians and a party that espoused the most radical political, social, judicial, and economic policies. Abortion advocacy, which includes the heinous practice of partial-birth abortion, the legalization of many forms of sexual deviancy, the rejection of God from their platform, silence on rising anti-Semitism in their midst, praising lawlessness at the borders, their endorsement of Socialism and Marxism, pushing uncontrolled spending on "social" programs, which ensnare entire populations of our country in a cycle of poverty, are all part of the Democrat Left's political platform. Even as I sit here writing I scratch my head as to how this is possible. I read the Bible and teach it regularly and I study it in depth in my research and writing. At no point do I ever find the Bible endorsing or hinting at the acceptance of such godless positions. Yet here we are in 2021 looking at the chaos being generated by the Democrat party under a Biden-Harris administration. This was only made possible by a host of self-professing Christians voting for such a godless pair.

Due to these concerns, in this chapter I want to outline how so-called "liberal" Christians have not only gotten it wrong when it comes to their political leanings, they are in fact hastening God's judgment on America because of their lax understanding, either by omission or commission, of what the Bible teaches about personal responsibility and key social issues.

The Main Concern

Already there may be some questioning my motives for writing such an indictment. I am sure there will be some who will call me partisan, a sore loser because of the 2020 outcome, or what have you. The truth is I simply cannot wrap my head around the concept of a "liberal" Christian, an oxymoron in my thinking and understanding of the Bible. What would cause someone to think that voting for these types of policies was biblical? I know, I know, many will say, "Brian, you are naïve and do not understand that Jesus was a socialist who was always on the side of the outcast and underdog. The Democrats are the party also of the downtrodden and therefore we must support their candidates." Although I have handled this topic in detail in my last book titled *The Bible, Sexuality, and Culture*, I do want to note briefly here that such argumentation is problematic on its face. First, it is a fallacy to believe that the Right is against the downtrodden. Those on the Right simply believe that personal responsibility must also play a key role in aiding those who need help. Second, any party that espouses lawlessness and policies antithetical to the Bible is not a party with which Jesus would be aligned. Jesus is not going to contradict the teaching of the Torah especially when it comes to social issues. Third, while I realize Jesus did not come as a political leader (the first time), he certainly would not have associated himself with a party built on greed for power,[12] unforgiveness, and yes, one that supports social movements like BLM and Antifa that are race baiting and economically jealous of those who have more than they do. It is important to point out that BLM is not just rooted in Marxist ideology, those at the highest level say it is a spiritual movement, one that practices necromancy-like rituals to conjure the spirits of those who they say were unjustly killed at the hand of their oppressors.[13] Finally, Jesus was not a "socialist." He was a Jewish male who endorsed a political ideology based upon the theocratic teachings of the Torah. At no point does the Torah reject personal property and wealth. What it rejects is abusing the poor to gain that wealth as well as a person's unwillingness to help the poor in their midst. I find it telling that one of the only times when Jesus could have endorsed a social-istic ideology, he rejected it. Let me explain. When a man approached Jesus and asked him to force his brother to share his inheritance, Jesus refused to get involved but instead called out the greed of the man (Luke 12:13–15). Jesus then used this encounter to launch into a par-able instructing on the dangers of greed (Luke 12:16–20). Whatever the reason may be for a Christian to vote for godless policies, it can never be justified if those policies are leading the nation towards judgment, and that, my friend, is where we as a nation are heading.

Why is this important to my ongoing thesis? It is vital for two main reasons. First, Christians are responsible for who they place in positions of power. The author of Proverbs notes that "righteousness exalts a nation, but sin is a reproach to any people" (Prov 14:34; my translation). When we elect leaders, who endorse godless policies, we are hastening God's judgment upon our nation. Now I realize that the Right has its problems as well and I know that there are godless men and women on both sides. The difference is in how the Right and the Left view America. One sees it as founded upon Judeo-Christian ideals that are worth fighting for, preserving, and passing on to the next gen-eration. The other side views the American "experiment" as a complete and utter failure and in need of revision according to modern thinking and secular humanistic ideology devoid of God and biblical influence (I will return to this concept in a later chapter). Second, Christians who continue to support godlessness through their voting patterns are not only hastening the downward spiral of our nation, but their actions may also be betraying what is in their heart. This can either be a naiveté of the facts they are espousing, or the hubris that they know better than God. The latter position is a scary place in which to reside. God's Word is eternal and is perfect in its instruction for human flourishing.

Unfortunately, too many "elite" Christians, evangelicals in particular, feel that the Church has misunderstood and misinterpreted the Bible to the detriment of sexual minorities and the downtrodden. This is a topic too broad to handle here but I would direct my readers to my other works dealing with these topics.[14]

What I will say is that as someone who has studied the Bible extensively, I know when political policies are unbiblical. And I also know that while we need to be irenic to our Christian brothers and sisters, those who are intransigent in their thinking and who consistently support anti-biblical policies and a party that is vocally anti-God, have moved away from the faith and are in danger of judgment (Matt 7:15; John 8:44–45; James 3:1; 1 John 2:19). America's problem is not just its lack of a fear of God, it is a lack of the fear of God by some of those at the highest levels of the Church. As such I am calling them out for their godlessness. In this regard, we must remember that both Paul and Jesus reserved some of their harshest critiques for the religious elite of their day (Matt 6:2, 5, 16; 23:27; Phil 3:2; Gal 1:8–9 etc.). In the next portion of this chapter, I want to look at three different areas where the liberal elites of the Church have gotten it wrong.

Where Liberal Christianity Has Gotten It Wrong: The Blight of Abortion

Democrats championed the 1973 *Roe v. Wade* decision, and the Democrat party made pro-choice policies part of their party platform. Although America is responsible as a nation, the institution and elevation of this heinous practice is to be placed squarely on the shoulders of the Democrat party and their feminist allies.[15] As I noted in my previous chapter, God will judge any nation that sheds innocent blood. Abortion is a stain on our nation that will not be removed by a few people repenting of individual infractions. Judgment is coming because we as a nation, and as a Church, have allowed it to be perpetuated for so long with little to no pushback from Christians, especially by those who identify as "liberal." I once heard it stated that every abortion clinic should have a sign over its door that reads "Here by permission of the Church." Indeed, our silence will be our undoing. For those of us who have attempted to change policy but have been thwarted by liberal Christians because of their voting patterns, the blood of the unborn is on their heads. Allow me to offer a poignant reminder of the spiritual blindness and political stupidity of those in the "liberal" Christian camp.

Leading up to the 2020 election I saw a disturbing website with the title, "Pro-Life Evangelicals for Biden." The creators of the website boasted several "movers and shakers" in the evangelical world of academia, public speaking, and publishing, as coming out in support of Biden. Many, I am sure, thought that this was a good way to rally other evangelicals to abandon Trump and side with a "respectable" alternative; one who would be more "suitable" for the "conscientious" Christian voter. Many used the tired and misinformed mantra of supporting "all life from the womb to the tomb" as the reason for their support of the Biden-Harris ticket. In many of the swing states where Biden "won" by a few thousand votes, these evangelicals were key in putting Biden into office. They actually thought he was going to be a moderate. Instead, they got exactly what he said he was: a pro-abortion candidate who would do everything in his power to increase this heinous practice. Not surprisingly, Biden was true to his word to what he had promised his radical base. Within the first two months of Biden's presidency, he disappointed his "pro-life evangelical" supporters by refusing to enforce the long-standing Hyde Amendment, which outlawed the use of taxpayer monies to fund abortion. Now these same duped evangelicals have sent the President an open letter from their group "Pro-life Evangelicals for Biden" stating that they feel used.[16] It is obvious that the Enemy used these naïve evangelicals as "useful idiots" to foster more killing of the unborn. To be sure, numerous websites have reported the outrage (whether their outrage is real or feigned is another matter) of those from this camp who had supported Biden but now feel betrayed.[17] What did these so-called believers expect? Can a leopard change its spots? The Democrat party has made it clear that they support abortion up to the point of birth and now include allowing infanticide for botched abortions. Again, while I am sure there may have been a few of these naïve evangelicals who actually thought that Biden would go against his radical base and support pro-life policies for the unborn, the truth is that many of the liberal elite voted for Biden because they themselves are liberal! Some may have been simply trying to justify their vote to the rest of the Christian world, while others were attempting to shame those on the Right for supporting the purported "tyranny" of Trump.

Where Liberal Christianity Has Gotten It Wrong: Hatred for Trump and His Supporters

Judgment on America *and* the Church is certain when self-professing evangelicals become so blind with hate for Trump, the Right, and for sound god-fearing policies that they endorse a radical duo like Biden and Harris (and Obama and Clinton of the past). The Church is so divided that many on the Left preferred to elect a Nero figure to persecute the Church as opposed to electing a Cyrus figure who would bless the people of God. During the election cycle of 2020, Nero for many was more acceptable because he was a "nice" grandfatherly figure who spoke the things they wanted to hear. As noted above, this was all a ruse and many liberal Christians fell into the trap. Now America is in a quandary as we navigate through the turmoil unfolding in almost every area of the administration's monetary, public and international policies, and social agenda.

There is a clear biblical example of this type of chaos and political blindness. We need to keep in mind that sometimes God gives a nation exactly what they want. Saul is a case in point. When the people of Israel no longer wanted the aged Samuel as their leader, they demanded change. They did not like the way the country of Israel was going (see 1 Samuel 8). Instead of listening to God's prophet, they decided they wanted a king over them so they could be like the nations. God told Samuel to give the people what they wanted so he gave them Saul. Initially Saul appeared to be the right choice, but in the end, he turned out to be a tyrant who hunted down God's true choice for king—David

THE GATHERING STORM · 37

—as well as his followers. The parallels are striking in that today the Democrat Left is doing everything in its power to destroy Trump, even after he is out of office, as well as his followers. The fiasco of January 6, 2021 is being used as a pretext to make examples of anyone who would dare to stand up to the tyranny of the Left, especially when it comes to the questionable outcomes of a supposed "perfect" election. Ironically, where Saul had at least a few years of a "honeymoon" period with Israel, Biden and Harris wasted no time wrecking the US economy and undermining the social fabric of America. Within the first formative 100 days of his administration, a *Washington Post* poll showed that Biden ranked among the bottom two American presidents since Eisenhower with the lowest net approval (difference between approval and disapproval).[18] As I write, he is "underwater" with approval ratings in the 30 percentile.

Another disturbing trend is the fact that the liberal elite evangelical "Christians" hate the religious conservative Right more than they hate sin and the devil. They would rather see the devil have full reign of our nation than to ever have a Donald Trump or someone like him in office ever again. I have read numerous essays and books full of vitriol that were published after Trump's 2016 victory. According to these "elites" (their own terminology) the "uneducated" and "smelly Walmart shoppers" were the ones who put the travesty of Trump into office, and they made no bones about letting us all know their disapproval of the "racist" tendencies of the conservative Christian Right. This type of hatred and antagonism was also on display during the final year of the Trump presidency. Indeed, liberal Christianity's hatred of Trump supporters has been painfully evident in how they responded to conservative churches in the midst of the recent Covid crisis. My wife, Christine, will speak directly to this issue next.

Where Liberal Christianity Has Gotten It Wrong: They have Become the State Church

As a life-long Episcopal turned Anglican, I, Christine, feel I can speak directly to what I am witnessing in the mainline churches. A few years ago, it seemed like every other Christian book being published was about Dietrich Bonhoeffer (1906–1945) or at least made references to him. Bonhoeffer was a German theologian who was part of the more conservative Confessing Church during WWII. In 2011, Eric Metaxas wrote his biography, and soon others followed with different interpretations of various aspects of his theology. As people's awareness of Bonhoeffer rose, it felt as if everyone wanted to be him. And, to be honest, who wouldn't? He is clearly a giant of the faith, and a person to appreciate for standing true to his convictions in the face of state control and the complicity and silence of the German state church. He chose hardship to combat Nazism, and in the end faced his own death for his stand. Bonhoeffer was executed in the closing days of WWII by the Germans for being a part of a plot to assassinate Hitler. The fact is, even though everyone imagines himself as a Bonhoeffer, if we were faced with similar circumstances, most of us are not. If we are honest with ourselves, we have more of the state church tendencies than we would like to admit.

I was particularly struck with how easily swayed those of us in the Church have been with the Covid-19 fiasco. After the initial shock and fear of this virus, some more conservative churches sought to open their doors. I completely understand why churches closed their doors initially. We did not understand the virus, and we thought this would be a temporary bump in the road. When churches did take the brave step of opening, many were met with opposition. While I expected opposition from *outside* the Church, I was dismayed by the number of voices *inside* the Church urging people to stay at home. Paul clearly instructs the Church not to forsake the gathering of the faithful, and yet here we are doing just that. And no, zoom meetings do not count. They are mere stop gaps and do not fulfill the need so many of us have to congregate in person.

The sad truth is that the majority of people I see advocating for staying at home seem to be coming from the more liberal side of the Church. This seems particularly poignant in two examples from our neighboring country to the north. When an Albertan pastor was jailed for having church services, members of the clergy from other denominations, the Anglican church included, wrote him a letter chastising him for holding services and somehow besmirching the name of Jesus for not following the dictates of the state. Then, another Albertan pastor, who came from communist Ukraine, demanded that the Royal Canadian Mounted Police leave his church on Good Friday and allow his flock to worship in peace. A few weeks later he was arrested in the middle of the highway for continuing to hold services. Again, clergy from liberal denominations decried this man's un-Christlike behavior for not following the state's recommendations.

Church, we have ceded much to the State. We have ceded to the government care for the poor, care for the sick, education, and even to a certain extent, what constitutes morality. We have grown comfortable with this arrangement, reassuring ourselves by claiming that we need to focus on winning souls. We need both. Souls need food, shelter, and education. Souls need a place to gather, to hear the Word, admonish each other, and to offer a physical presence. Liberal and conservative churches have been both found wanting in this pandemic, but those who advocate for continued lock downs, mostly from the liberal side, seem to miss the value of the corporate body of the Church. They walk in lock step with the State and are proud to do so.

I, Brian, want to add to my wife's insights by noting a final troubling encounter between a mother and a Catholic priest and bishop in Texas.[19] Shortly after Texas began to reopen from the pandemic, a family went to their local church for Mass. When the pregnant mother refused to wear a mask because her infant child continued to pull it off her face, the priest called the police on her. She and her family were confronted by police and removed from the service. Later, the bishop of the diocese stood with the decision of the priest to call the police on his parishioner. The Church once again showed its true colors of siding with the State and against a follower of God.

Conclusion

In the above discussion we have only scratched the surface of the problems America is facing due to the complete failure of the liberal church to stand united with faithful Christians on the Right in their fight to stand for God's Word and its teaching and to ward off coming judgment. We did not even mention the numerous ways the elite liberal church is undermining the cause of Christ with their support for ungodly and unbiblical social and sexual agendas. On the latter point we offer a word of warning. For those who are truly God-fearing but are still aligned with liberal churches or who support the political Left, if you are thinking that you will be spared from the juggernaut of the sexual revolution and the agendas of the Left because of your support for *most* of their policies, you are wrong. When the State and the Church become married in an unholy alliance like we are seeing with mainline churches and the Left, any voice that attempts to sound an alarm from within that "state" church will be silenced. We offer one recent example of the coming onslaught. In Finland two Bible-believing Christians (one a former member of parliament and one a bishop elect) are being charged with hate speech for holding to the biblical model for sexuality and for standing up against the LGBTQ agenda. For this in-excusable slight against "unity" and for their "discrimination" both are facing up to six years of prison time unless they recant.[20] In one case, all the person did was post a picture on social media of Paul's teaching from Romans 1 on sexual sin. She added nothing to the post. For this she is being punished for a hate crime. While most conservatives would recoil at such a travesty, based upon what we are witnessing in America and Canada, we are not overly optimistic that the liberal branch of Christianity will be too heartbroken and empathetic of those on the Right who take a stand. For this reason, the liberal church has become a part of the problem and their unholy alliance with the State, particu-larly the Left, is sure to hasten God's judgment on America.

5

❦

Atmospheric Disturbances: The Lawless One Spreads Lawlessness

In meteorology, tornadoes, cyclones, hurricanes, and the like, all fall into the category of atmospheric disturbances and can bring dangerous conditions on the ground that cause vast destruction to those who are unfortunate enough to be in their path. As part of a thunderstorm, lightening can strike at any moment and bring great destruction. Atmospheric disturbances like thunderstorms are caused by the collision of high and low pressure systems. Today, in America, we are experiencing the collision of two metaphorical "pressure systems" which is bringing chaotic conditions. One pressure system is focused on law and order and based upon historical Judeo-Christian norms while the other is rooted in lawlessness and disorder and seeks to undermine every facet of our Judeo-Christian foundation. At the root of the latter is the father of lawlessness, the devil (John 8:44–45). Not surprisingly, when atmospheric disturbances lead to fierce storms, one of the side effects is often a breakdown in law and order as police themselves struggle to deal with the natural disaster. I would remind my reader of what happened to law and order in the aftermath of Hurricane Katrina when it struck Louisiana. Looting was the norm. What we are experiencing today in America is nothing short of spiritual atmospheric disturbances, brought about by the Enemy. The Enemy brings not only spiritual and cultural destruction, but lawlessness in general. Ironically, Jesus said to his disciples when speaking of hubris, "I saw Satan fall from heaven as lightening" (Luke 10:18).

Peter tells us that the devil is out to seek and destroy humanity (1 Peter 5:8). Part of that plan is to lead people away from the truth both with a small "t" and Truth with a capital "T," namely, Jesus. Jesus made this clear when he said, "I am the Way, the Truth, and the Life, and no person comes to the Father except through me" (John 14:6; my paraphrase). There are many ways that the Enemy comes to lead people astray and to entice them to reject God's Truth. One of those ways is to spread confusion. Paul states plainly that God is not the author of confusion (1 Cor 14:33) thus intimating that the devil is. When we look around our nation and see chaos and confusion at all levels it does not take a rocket scientist to figure out that this type of behavior is not from God. Now do not get me wrong, because we live in a fallen world, chaos can happen naturally. To be sure, hurricanes, tornados, earthquakes, and the like are all means of bringing chaos into the world (Rom 8:22). However, this is not the chaos and confusion on which I want to focus. The Enemy has fostered and laid the groundwork for cultural confusion and lawlessness in America. We have made this possible *because* we have rejected God. Although we have always suffered from chaotic times, and, yes, even lawlessness (I am thinking of the 1960s), what America is experiencing today is not lawlessness at the periphery or fringes of culture and society, but rather lawlessness at all levels of society, from the "top" (politically speaking) all the way down to the nuclear family.

In this chapter I want to examine some of the various ways we can identify how the Enemy is spreading lawlessness in our country. What we are seeing are the symptoms of a nation devoid of God and on a collision course with God's judgment because of our rejection of his righteous dictates. The Enemy is using the Left as well as Christian complacency to bring about lawlessness thus pushing our country towards judgment. The rise of Marxism is a primary example.

The Marxist Takeover

The ultimate form of lawlessness is a rejection of God and his mandates. For the past sixty years or more, there has been a concerted effort within America to remove God from the public square, from the houses of Congress, and from daily American life. One of the ways this has been accomplished is through education, which in turn has affected public policy through the next generation of leaders. The radical Marxists of the 1960s, and now their followers, are currently in all areas of power. What they knew they could not do through a violent revolution in the 60s has been accomplished, almost completely without bloodshed (in this regard, Antifa and BLM certainly cross the line regularly). Our society has accepted socialism and Marxist ideology because of their time in the ivory towers of academia. Millennials and Generation Z are completely indoctrinated, thus, as of 2022, we are in the final throes of the takeover.

Scholars have noted that there are four key steps to any Marxist takeover. These include: 1) Propaganda to demoralize culture; 2) Destabilization of the culture; 3) Repeated manufacturing of crises to continue the destabilization; and 4) The normalization of the chaos and the status quo by heralding it as the new "normal."[21] We have witnessed this with ever-increasing regularity during the past decade or more. The Marxists have done this in an effort to manipulate and program Americans to do as they are told while relying on the government for their wellbeing and the solutions to their problems. One Democrat operative, Rahm Emanuel, famously stated, "Do not let a crisis go to waste." Of course, this was straight out of Saul Alinsky's book *Rules for Radicals* which he dedicated to Lucifer.[22] This alone should be enough to end the debate for the believer when it comes to the plan of the Left, but too many are ignorant of history and the lawlessness of Marxism.

Others simply refuse to educate themselves because the old adage, "Ignorance is bliss," has become their mantra. Marxism is anti-God and fosters a complete rejection of American Judeo-Christian ideology. Not surprisingly, Marxism is also the ideology adopted by the likes of BLM and Antifa. Some have even left BLM because of their horrid ideology.[23] Sadly, Marxist ideology often wrapped in the guise of BLM and Antifa activism is now pervasive in our schools as well.

God's judgment is coming because of the Church's rejection of sound doctrine and because of our failure to withstand and counteract the indoctrination of our children. Now our children are coming home from universities across America indoctrinated with an ideology that is anti-God and anti-America. The Enemy knows that a nation divided against itself will not stand (Matt 12:25). He has done his work well. America will not survive unless God intervenes, and Christians begin to take back the ground we ceded to the Enemy. This includes not just the church, but politics, media, the arts, and any other enterprise or institution usurped by the Left.

The Lawlessness of the Education System

Several surveys and studies have been done over the past few years highlighting the lawlessness within our education system.[24] Much of this has to do with the fact that liberal and leftist ideology now is the norm within the education system. Back in the 1950s the liberal to conservative ratio of college professors was close to an even split (3 to 2), with a slight tilt to the Left. Today those numbers are closer to 8 to 1 liberal to conservative with some departments, like the humanities and social sciences, reaching 11 to 1 or higher.[25] The reason this is important is not just the fact that there is virtually no debate on the moral trajectory of our education system now that the Left has a complete death grip on the academy, but rather that the leftists in these departments are increasingly embracing Marxist ideology, which is being propagated to our vulnerable students. Even in conservative areas of the country, the teachers' union has a monopoly on education and within that union, the vast majority are liberal. Again, to show how bad it is, one "study of 7,243 professors in economics, law, psychology, history, and journalism/communication at the 40 top-rated universities found that 66 of 170 departments surveyed had no Republican faculty members at all. Zero."[26] The Enemy has hijacked the public school system from K-12 and the publicly funded universities as well.[27]

Susie or Johnny, who left home as respectable conservative, God-fearing, and patriotic children, are returning home as hostile, radical, and ungrateful "aliens" in our homes and country at large. Critical race theory is now being pushed to deepen the division between the races while fostering a deep hatred for each other and for the founding of our country. You may think I am being extreme but all one has to do is turn on the news and see young people rioting in the streets and burning down the inner cities. Marxist and leftist ideology is now being pedaled at younger and younger ages and has found its way into all branches of government the military included. So now you cannot even send your child to the military to get "straightened out" on the value of hard work, patriotism, and respect for authority. Instead, the Left is turning this once respectable institution into a "woke" testing ground for a future Marxist revolution whereby the army will fall into lockstep with the governing powers. Not only is the army now beginning to purge "undesirables" (code for Trump supporters) at the behest of the Democrats,[28] but it has adopted the LGBTQ agenda. The latter is clearly on display by the new recruitment ad put out by the Army promoting LGBTQ lifestyles.[29] The irony of ironies is that while the Taliban marched across Afghanistan, the US military was flying the Pride flag over their base in Kabul. Not surprisingly this did not sit well with the Taliban when they swept into the city. This reality should be frightening for every American. It is a direct threat to our Constitutional Republic when the Left seeks to hijack the power of the military. I will address this further in a later chapter on totalitarianism.

In response to the lawlessness at all levels of the education system, some parents are pushing back against the chaos by turning to home-schooling. Prior to the Covid-19 pandemic three percent of Americans homeschooled their children. Now eleven percent of families have turned to this as an option to counter the Left's attacks. I realize that in many cases, parents may not have this as an option. Because of this, parents need to be ready to counter the indoctrination of the Left with solid instruction at home. The mobilization of parents across America to take back their schoolboards is encouraging, but make no mistake, the leftists in the teachers' unions will not give up power easily or without a legal fight. The weaponization of the Department of Justice and the FBI to go after parents who are voicing their concerns at school-board meetings and labeling them as "domestic terrorists" is the first of many attacks sure to follow at the behest of the powerful unions. What is more, even homeschooling is not as safe as it once was. If the leftists have their way, homeschooling will be outlawed, and all children will be forced into government indoctrination institutions. Academics are already pushing for this very thing.[30]

Immigration Gone Awry

Back in the eighth century, the Assyrian Empire under Shalmaneser V (727–722 BC) and his successor, Sargon II (722–705 BC), continued a policy against Israel which the Assyrians had used as a means of controlling conquered populations (2 Kgs 17:1–6; 18:9–11). The Assyrians would remove conquered nations and transplant them to a new region/country in order to remove any nationalistic pride from conquered foes. It also served as an excellent deterrent to remove any desire of the conquered nation to fight back to protect their own land against the invaders. The conquered peoples simply became a part of the Assyrian collective. God used the Assyrians as a means of bringing judgment upon Israel. The natural outcome of the Assyrian policy was that the new peoples who had been brought into Israel did not know the ways and traditions of their new land, and God in turn brought judgment upon them for profaning God's holy land (2 Kgs 17:25–26). In response to this chaos, the Assyrian king had one of the Israelite priests return from captivity and teach the new immigrants the ways of God even though it had little effect because the foreign populations brought their own gods with them (2 Kgs 17:27–28). Put simply, this period was a time of chaos in the land of Israel as a foreign population replaced native Israelites. This led to conflict between the people of God in Judah and this new population. The interlopers did not have the same respect for the ways and customs of Israel as the native population had.

Today, the Left is doing to America exactly what the Assyrians did to other nations. They are using illegal immigration as a means of removing national identity and hence the people's desire to stand and fight for America's distinctives. To be sure, the leftist elites are doing this as we speak with unfettered immigration and with an "open-borders" policy. Antifa and BLM protest in the streets chanting "No borders, no walls, no USA at all."[31] And we have witnessed illegal immigrants storming the border waving the flags, not of America, but of the countries of their origins. We are witnessing entire regions of cities and states being overrun with immigrants who refuse to assimilate to their new home but instead bring the baggage of undemocratic principles with them. I am not anti-immigrant: I am one myself. What I am against is unfettered immigration, which is rooted in lawlessness. What is happening on the US southern border is a travesty and the epitome of lawlessness. And the Democrats are fanning the flames for more. This is not of God.

The Democrats often suggest they are pro-immigrant because of their supposed compassion for the poor, but this is a ruse. I guarantee you that if most immigrants voted Republican, the Democrats would be passing legislation to build a wall a mile high with Nancy Pelosi and Chuck Schumer there helping to build it. Clear evidence of this reality came in July 2021, when the Biden administration refused to allow Cuban immigrants, who were fleeing the unrest of the Cuban riots, to enter the US despite allowing hundreds of thousands of illegal border crossers to continue unimpeded on the southern border. The reason for the double standard? Cubans overwhelmingly vote Republican because they know the dangers of Communist and Marxist rule in Cuba. But for those coming from Central America, this is not always the case because statistics clearly show that these immigrants tend to vote Democrat because of government handouts and the government's turning of a blind eye to their illegal entrance into the country in the first place. For Democrats, illegal immigration is first and foremost about getting votes and building a coalition of minorities to hold power indefinitely and displace conservative American voters.[32] But there is more at play in their policies. The Left with its Marxist values is seeking the destruction of America and its Judeo-Christian ideals and foundation. They want to remake the nation in their image (that is, godless). Lawlessness is just one of the traits of the Enemy and we are witnessing it unfold before our eyes.

Lance Wallnau is certainly correct to note that God establishes nations. Now, whether they are sheep or goat nations depends on their acceptance of God's ideals. Whatever the case may be, one cannot get past the fact that clearly defined nations with borders are the plan of God (Deut 32:8; Matt 25:32–33).[33] The Left wants a collective with a one-world-government mentality. Again, the Bible is clear that this is not God's plan. When humanity rebelled by congregating in one place at the Tower of Babel God dispersed them (Gen 11:9). Not surprisingly, the end time ruler, the Antichrist, will attempt to once more unite humanity in the quest for world dominance (Rev 13; see more in Chapter 11). It is important for Believers to recognize that the Democrat policies of open borders is planned and calculated to bring about a desired outcome. It is evident that in the process to amass power and prestige by welcoming foreigners, the intended consequence will be the erasure of a distinct America, one that continues in Judeo-Christian fundamentals. The Left and those advocating for a weak border help to usher in a weakened US as well. It is also another example of why coming judgment is assured. The Enemy is in control and is attempting to bring America to its knees. He is using the Left to displace the old guard, who believe in the American Judeo-Christian way. The Left also knows that illegal immigrants will continue to vote for their lawless policies. This is evident in the Left's attempt to undermine our electoral process by allowing anyone to vote, including the illegals that the Democrats allow to cross our borders unfettered. Right now, in New York City, the Democrats are pushing to allow 800,000 illegal immigrants to vote in local elections, a first step in allowing them to vote federally.

The Lawlessness of America's Elections

Lawlessness is not just confined to the liberal elites' refusal to enforce the laws of the land, or activist groups roaming the streets, or to the destructive and nebulous political ideologies of the Left. It is also manifest more tangibly in how we as a nation allow our elections to be run. Improper election procedures and the corruption of the election system will be the undoing of our nation. Indeed, a quick overview of political takeovers by dictators and tyrants in recent history shows that the primary way they came to power was through the corruption or complete overthrow of the democratic election process. I would offer Russia, Venezuela, Germany of the 1930s, and various Banana Republics as prime examples. When election integrity is lost, people no longer vote. As a result, those usurping the system move forward with impunity to rule with an iron fist.

As touched on in my Introduction, what I witnessed in the 2020 election as a newly minted US citizen was nothing less than devastating to my vision of America. I remember watching on election night and the days following as Democrat, BLM, and Antifa thugs intimidated and, in many cases, forcefully removed the opposition from counting rooms and polling precincts. It was like I was watching a third-world country feign an election. I thought at the time that this would never stand, and that the judiciary would get involved and overturn election results in at least these key locations where blatant violations of election law was being perpetrated. I would come to realize that there was no judicial will to do so. Whether this was due to the Left's intimidation, or because of conflicting political ideologies within the judiciary, or a combination of both, one may never know. With a year now past since the election, nothing has been done to bring to justice those responsible for the lawlessness during the 2020 election.

I never followed political election "theater" too closely but that changed since November of 2020. In the aftermath of the lawlessness of November 3rd I came to realize that many states had changed election laws, many against the will of Republican-run state houses. Rogue Secretaries of State (many funded by the Left), illegal rulings by activist judges and state supreme courts, the usurping of the rights of state legislators, backroom consent decrees, illegal actions by local election officials and county clerks, among a host of other issues, and straight up fraud, tilted the election in the favor of Democrats.

Why is this important to my thesis of God's judgment on America? It is important because this type of activity is the hallmark of the Enemy and the lawlessness that accompanies dictatorial takeovers. We are no longer talking about focused cheating like that of the infamous Chicago Mayor Daley for John F. Kennedy in 1960. On the contrary, we are talking about a wide and concerted effort to game the election system nationwide for the benefit of one party. Trump was accused of being a dictator, yet the Left was merely transferring onto the President what *they* always do. They brought about a complete usurpation of the electoral process and then later bragged about how they did it by calling it the "fortification" of the election to "save America" so Trump would lose.[34] They were not even trying to hide their lawlessness. When our nation, which was founded upon Judeo-Christian values, the rule of law, and the throwing off of tyrannous government, turns around and fosters tyranny in our elections, judgment cannot be too far behind. As I noted in my earlier chapters, too many left-leaning Christians hailed the election as completely secure and sided with the radical Left because their "guy" had won. But this is yet one more step down the road to God's judgment. When injustice and lawlessness is allowed to stand, a nation will not long endure.

The full repercussions of the 2020 election have not been felt yet but early indications point in a direction that will include more, not less, lawlessness. A party that decried the executive orders of Trump as dictatorial, outstripped him by having Biden sign dozens within his first few days in office. Threats of packing SCOTUS and other court jurisdictions is bantered around as a means of getting laws passed that the Democrats cannot pass legislatively. Of course, there is also the threats of adding states to give the Left more votes in the Senate and House. And I have already noted the blatant overreach of the Democrats to federalize elections with their HR1 bill and to legislate Christian institutions to accept the Left's sexual agenda with the "Equality Act" known as HR5. Recently the Democrats attempted to enforce vaccine mandates for all private companies with one hundred employees or more by weaponizing OSHA. While this attempt at coercion was partially struck down by SCOTUS as unconstitutional, there can be no doubt that the Left is testing the waters for complete control of our lives. This is not about health; this is about complete control and submission to the will of the State (see more in Chapter 7). While the Left has always been aggressive, what we are witnessing in the past few months is nothing less than breathtaking in its sweep and speed. Even some Democrats are wondering what is going on with some even apologizing to Republicans for voting for Biden and Harris.[35] Lawlessness will be the undoing of America and nowhere is this more apparent than in what is happening daily in our streets.

Lawlessness in the Streets

For more than a year now, America has experienced upheaval on the streets of many urban centers, especially those cities where Democrats control all branches of government. Antifa and BLM rioters roam the streets burning, looting, and in some cases, murdering innocent people at will. The lawlessness of these groups and the refusal of Democrat-run city and state officials to prosecute the perpetrators is further evidence that America is slipping into a period of judgment. Liberal calls to defund the police have been enacted in some cities with devastating effects. From 2020 to 2021 alone several Democrat-run cities have seen double digit increases in violent crime and murder. For example, as of May 25, 2021, New York City and Chicago were up 22 percent, Los Angeles was up 27 percent, Washington DC jumped 35 percent, Philadelphia increased 40 percent, Minneapolis increased 56 percent, and

Portland, Oregon, had a whopping 800 percent increase.[36] Anarchy is not the hallmark of blessing; it is just the opposite. Since the uprising of these two domestic terrorist groups (BLM and Antifa), governments have been paralyzed with fear in how to deal with them. Most of the time police arrest the criminals while corrupt District Attorneys drop all charges and quietly release them back onto the streets to perpetrate the same crimes again. Politicians have turned a blind eye to all the carnage and chaos. For example, during the 2020 election cycle as many inner-city communities were ablaze, Biden erroneously propounded that Antifa was an "idea," not an organized resistance. Kamala Harris even lobbied for people to contribute to a fund to bail out the BLM and Antifa thugs so they could return to their vandalism. Such oblivion and flouting of law are further evidence that we have lost our way.

Closely connected to the lawlessness in the streets is the inequity in punishments and justice for those on the wrong side of the political aisle. We have watched as Antifa and BLM rioters and terrorists get a pass because they represent the corruption on the Left and are the "brown shirts" and militant arm of the Democrat party while those who entered the capital on January 6, 2021, sit rotting in jails, some in solitary confinement. What we are witnessing is a bifurcated judicial system that favors the Left and punishes the Right. One need to look no further than the silence on Hunter Biden's antics and question-able international dealings compared to how Donald Trump's children were treated for the most minor of trumped-up infraction (no pun intended). Or consider the way Trump's business dealings were scruti-nized compared to the complete oblivious behavior of the MSM and the intelligence community concerning the glaring conflicts of inter-est between Joe Biden's business dealings with China and the foreign slush fund he has with the University of Pennsylvania.[37] And Hunter Biden's so-called art sales to foreign dignitaries are a blatant example of the corrupt double standard. America cannot stand with prevalent and openly flouted injustice. Indeed, when laws are passed codifying sexual proclivities of all types and the President's son gets a pass for questionable sexual acts, we are witnessing another bridge that we have crossed and burned to ashes behind us as a nation.

The Lawlessness of America's Sexual Ethics

Recently one of my former professors, Tiberius Rata, made a statement that stuck with me. He said, "We were always told that you cannot legislate morality and meanwhile we legislated immorality." Nothing demonstrates the lawlessness of a culture more than the uncontrolled sexual practices and proclivities of a nation's inhabitants. While I have handled this topic in book-length format in *The Bible, Sexuality, and Culture* (2021), here I want to highlight just a few examples to prove my point that America's sexual ethics is not the representation of a liberated society, but rather is evidence of natural lawlessness, and more specifically, a rejection of God's laws, which will certainly hasten God's judgment.

According to a recent Gallup poll, the sexual perversion of younger generations is not diminishing, but rather it is on the rise. The poll showed that 11.5 percent of Generation Z (18–23 years of age) now identify as bisexual, that is, the "B" in the acronym LGBTQ (Lesbian, Gay, Bisexual, Transexual, Questioning). Of the entire population who identify as LGBTQ, 72 percent of them identify as bisexual with half of those in the same group from the Millennial age group (24–39 years old) identifying as bisexual.[38] The laws of the Bible that state that sexual activity is to be between a man and a woman has been thrown out the proverbial window in favor of personal choice and perverse passions (Rom 1:26–28). With such a rise in sexual deviance, God is certainly not going to allow America to continue undisciplined lest we forget what happened prior to the flood (Gen 6:1–4), and the judgment that fell on the cities of the plain of which Sodom and Gomorrah were chief (Gen 19).

The issue at stake is how the lawlessness of humanity is now becoming mainstream as the Enemy shoves the growing perversion in our faces daily. It invades all aspects of life. Cadbury's 2021 Easter ad, for example, showed two gay men "sharing" an Easter cream egg. In the commercial each of them is holding half of the same chocolate-covered egg in their mouth as though they are getting ready to kiss; the rest of the imagery is vile and tasteless (no pun intended).[39] Now, the gay community no longer hides its agenda. Recently the gay choir of San Francisco released a video declaring their plan out loud. They are "coming for your children" to indoctrinate them and they are laughing and singing about it proudly.[40] Now we know at least four of those singing this song are convicted sex offenders.[41] Thirty years ago, most Americans viewed the sexual proclivities of this new "norm" as shameful. God's judgment is assured unless we have a changed culture. But alas, I am not hopeful that this will happen because many in the Church now see gay sex as acceptable and "normal" behavior. According to one of the earliest Jewish commentaries on Genesis (*Genesis Rabbah* 26.5) God's judgment came upon the world in the days of Noah because men started writing wedding hymns for each other and for unions between men and beasts. And this commentary dates to AD 400, not 2015 or 2021!

This new LGBTQ sexual revolution has had the immediate effect of lessening procreation as well. Why have children when you can divorce sex from procreation and marriage through all forms of promiscuity and perverse sexual contact? Because of this shift from God's mandates of procreation, America and western cultures are now seeing an untenable decline in birthrates. At 1.6 children on average per family, America cannot sustain its population. The good news is that conservative Americans are having children while left-leaning Americans are not. The latter's heritage will perish but God-fearing Americans will see their families increase.[42] This does not, however, answer the immediate problem of population decline. Increased immigration may stabilize the population, but the loss of our values due to the failure of foreigners to integrate as Americans will cause a loss of our Judeo-Christian ideals (see above). In some ways, Leftist ideology will judge itself by their rejection of God's sexual ethics and procreation but if the Church continues to adopt the thinking and worldview of the Left, judgment is assured.

Where did this perversion of our sexual ethics and Leftist ideology begin? To be sure, most of these traits are in the hearts of fallen humanity (Jer 17:9; Matt 15:19); however, as touched on above, sexual wantonness and a rejection of procreation (to save the environment) are being fostered and taught in the school rooms and university lecture halls across America. We are doomed as a nation unless God changes the hearts of people at all levels of society and government.

Conclusion

If one were to stop and seriously brainstorm concerning the way the Left has promoted lawlessness within our once-great country, we could fill an entire book with examples of this one topic. It is a topic of vital importance because of the licentiousness that the Father of Lies desires to implant into every area of American values and traditions, not to mention in the heart of every individual. Some of the craziness of the Left and their rejection of reason falls into the realm of the absurd. I am reminded of the stupidity of Disney's decision to remove the Snow-White ride at Disney World because the prince kisses her without permission at the end of the movie. We can't have that in our woke society! While this is indeed an example of the Left's stupidity, at the same time it also demonstrates that changing cultural traditions and norms is just another form of the lawlessness. At a more serious level are the examples of the lawlessness of the judicial branch that refuses to enforce laws because it is not convenient to the desired outcome of a particular group, namely liberal Democrats. As touched on above, SCOTUS's recent refusal to hear any of the election integrity cases, and especially the egregious examples of election violations in Pennsylvania (and Georgia) are cases in point.[43] The reason for this lawlessness did not happen in a vacuum, it once again has been fostered in the halls of our universities and is praised by the liberal media. Anyone who embraces sane decisions and rejects disorder are crucified by the media, specifically the MSM propagating their brand of "truth" from virtually every news outlet in America. When we get to the point where justice and righteousness stands afar off and truth falls in the streets (Isa 54:19) because of a failed media, judgment is sure to come.

6

The Storm Chasers: Wicked! The Problem of Media Bias

Cambridge's online dictionary defines a storm chaser as "a person who follows extreme weather events such as violent storms in order to experience, photograph, or study them." Many times, these storm chasers put themselves into harm's way to supply the general populace with videos and pictures, as well as personal experiences of what it is like to encounter firsthand the chaos (and the calm—the eye of a hurricane) of storms. Like modern storm chasers, reporters are supposed to report to the rest of us what is really happening in the dangerous and fast-paced world in which we live. In some cases, like storm chasers, reporters have to put themselves in harm's way in order to get the "scoop" on wars, natural and human-made disasters, the problem of crime, and government overreach.

Over the past two decades I have become an avid news follower. One of my earliest memories about the news comes from a time when I was only a few years old. I can still recall seeing the news on the TV during the closing days of the Vietnam War. Every night my parents turned on the nightly news to find out what was going on in the world. Like everyone else, my parents relied on the news network reporters and anchors to report the truth fairly and accurately. Even though many of these TV personalities may have had a liberal bent to their political leanings, it was not overtly obvious to the average person watching. We all came to trust the reporting of the MSM in the heyday of the nightly news anchormen and women.

The role of the press was so important to the founding fathers of America that they enshrined it in the First Amendment, which reads, "Congress shall make no law respecting an establishment of religion or prohibiting the free exercise thereof; or abridging the freedom of speech, or of the press; or the right of the people peaceably to assemble, and to petition the Government for a redress of grievances." Unfortunately, the once-trusted estate of the network news channels has lost its luster and its trustworthiness. In some cases, it has become nothing more than the propaganda arm of one political side or another, but usually of one party.

In this chapter I want to examine how the MSM has moved from being an important source of information to becoming a part of the news cycle itself. This may not appear to be associated with God's judgment on America, but as we will see, the role that the MSM is playing in today's America is in fact a key part of the downfall of our once-great nation. It is being used to program Americans to accept the most egregious lies; deceptions that the Enemy is using to divide America and to hasten God's judgment.

The Rise of the "Fake News" Media

The phrase, "fake news" may have been around prior to the Trump era, but make no mistake, Donald J. Trump made the phrase famous. Anyone who watched the two election cycles of 2016 and 2020 will easily remember the numerous times Trump would point out the news media at the back of the room at his rallies and call them out for what they were: fake news. The crowds loved it and jeered at the media for being so blatantly biased and hellbent on bringing an end to Trump's candidacy, and later, his presidency. We have all seen the MSM montages that show dozens of so-called "reporters" and news anchors parroting the same statements and using the same language to describe what supposedly was the most current Trump atrocity.[44] Phrases like "threat to our Democracy," "Russian collusion," "White-supremacist," "Hitler/Nazi," "Constitutional crisis," and "this rises to the level of an impeachable offense" were repeated endlessly on the 24/7 news loop across newsrooms in America. Sadly, the uninformed portion of the American public were gullible enough to accept it as fact. As the German propaganda minister, Joseph Goebbels, once said, "If you tell a lie big enough and keep repeating it, people will eventually come to believe it."[45] The talking points of the left-leaning MSM sounded more like they came directly from the Democrat party—and no doubt many times did—than from independent reporting.

The all-out attacks on Trump and his followers before and after the 2016 election set a new benchmark of bias. Some news anchors actually went on the record and made statements saying that they could not report on the Trump presidency like other presidencies: they had to become a part of the "resistance" and therefore be vocal critics of everything he did. They justified this as a service to America in order to save the nation from the scourge of Trump. They became cheerleaders for the Left and the Democrat party as opposed to objective reporters of the news. The reporting from 2016–2020 proved this bias to be true when *The Washington Times* reported in August of 2020 that over 95 percent of broadcast news on Trump was negative.[46] No other president experienced such media vitriol. This is important not simply because it was unfair to one party or to the President himself, but rather because it brought to light the way news is disseminated in America. It has a bias that is no longer implicit; it is overt.

While the attacks against conservatives and Trump are an obvious blackmark on the MSM, nothing is more troubling than the suppression of the truth. This is even more disturbing because now the public cannot make informed political, economic, cultural, and even medical decisions. The MSM blackout of any refences to the prophylactic use of hydroxchloroquine and ivermectin during the Covid pandemic is a case in point. They had an agenda to hurt Trump's chances of getting reelected so any truth in Trump's claims about the treatment of Covid with hydroxychloroquine, and now ivermectin, had to be suppressed. The MSM also needed to peddle the fear associated with Covid to help the Democrats push for election reforms that would favor the Democrats so they could steal the election. Project Veritas documented this in a video, which reveals the role of CNN to keep Covid fears stoked.[47] Now, after Biden is in office, we are finding out that Trump and many doctors were correct: hydroxychloroquine and ivermectin are in fact effective treatments for Covid.

From the political perspective, Big Tech's censorship of the Hunter Biden laptop controversy caused many fence-sitting Democrats and Independents to vote for Biden. When the news began to trickle out after the 2020 election about what Biden and his son, Hunter, were actually doing in shaking down foreign governments by selling Biden's political influence, 17 percent of Democrats said they would not have voted for Biden.[48] Here is a prime example of the dangers America is facing because of the MSM bias. And new evidence has been revealed that for some time now Google's algorithms have been used to redirect those searching for conservative topics to the Left's propaganda and other disinformation promoting left-leaning agendas while discrediting conservative politicians and topics.[49] America is being set up to believe whatever the Enemy desires us to believe and to suppress the truth for a lie (Rom 1:18). The peddling of fear and false information is being used to program the uniformed masses while attacks on those who know the truth increase. It certainly sounds like an end-time's scenario to me. My wife and I personally watched this unfold in the church realm as the MSM demonized Christians who opposed Covid lockdowns. We saw a similar occurrence when the MSM attacked those who rejected the Covid vaccines. The duped masses attacked the other side as the "enemy" of science and of America because that is what they had been programmed to think and do. They have become hypnotized by the constant propaganda.

The MSM Hatred of the "Deplorables" and Love for Antifa and BLM

We must remember that the attacks on Trump were not just against the President, they were attacks against those who stood with him, the "deplorables," who "clung to their guns or religion," as Obama declared, the conservative Right, Christians included. Trump took the brunt of the attacks which were just as much aimed at us. Translation: this means that those of us who hold to the values of Scripture are now in the crosshairs of the liberal media. Instead of advocating for the downtrodden individual who has been harassed or jailed for speaking their mind, the MSM no longer speaks "truth to power," they praise the crushing of dissent used against the MSM's enemies. Again, a quick on-line search will reveal numerous cases. During the Covid-19 pandemic, the media sided with the Left and went after any church that chose to stay open because of their religious convictions. They used their media bully pulpit to badger religious leaders into conforming by labeling them "irresponsible" and "killers." I know this is true because it happened in my home church with the local media. In Canada and the US, immigrants who fled communist countries in Europe have fought against the shutdowns in an effort to warn Americans and Canadians about the dangers of totalitarianism (see more in Chapter 7), a reality they lived through in communist countries. Instead of siding with these underdogs and sounding the warning alarm, the media has become nothing more than propaganda disseminators for the liberal governments of Canada and America.

Similarly, during the rise of the radical hate groups BLM and Antifa, the media sided with these domestic terrorist groups and went after any conservative who attempted to resist their movements. The disingenuous reporting of the August 12, 2017, Charlottesville, Virginia tragedy is a clear example. Trump was vilified as a "white-supremacist" even though he vocally rejected and denounced their movement. The media conveniently edited out that part of Trump's speech, a hack job that has continued to gain traction across internet sites and is parroted by reporters nationwide even today. And, of course, who can forget the

2019 Washington, DC racist fiasco created by the MSM when one of the Covington Catholic High School boys stood his ground in the face of withering and vile racist harangues? Fortunately, CNN was brought to heel for their careless reporting but not before the lies they propagated circled the globe on social media. Also, leading up to the 2020 election, the MSM refused to call out the nightly violence and rioting by Antifa and BLM for what it was. Instead, they called the unrest "peaceful" protests as their reporters stood in front of burning buildings. Chaos and anarchy helped the MSM cause, namely, to make sure Trump was removed from office. As noted above, Project Veritas is one watchdog group that has used undercover videos to expose the collusion of the MSM with the Democrats for the purpose of ousting Trump from office by means of hyping false stories and false narratives about the BLM riots and Covid-19.[50] Objective news reporting in the MSM is dead and instead is now on par with the Maoist propaganda arm of the Chinese Communist Party (hereafter CCP).

The MSM Parallels with the CCP

It goes without saying that globalist elites seek to merge America with the rest of the world. Indeed, the influence of the CCP on our corporations, media of all types, athletes, and politicians is a foregone conclusion. Many in America are more than willing to sell out their country for a bigger paycheck, higher dividends, or simply because their corporation is "in bed" with the CCP. Back in the days of McCarthy, communism was equivalent to a proverbial four-lettered word. The media agreed, for the most part, with this sentiment. Today, that is not the case. The MSM jovially reports about athletes, politicians, and corporations bowing to the CCP in an effort to win acceptance from this wicked and dangerous regime, a regime that mandates forced abortions, crushes any unacceptable speech or dissent (e.g., Hong Kong), commits genocide of oppressed populations within their borders (the Uyghurs), and imprisons Christians at a record pace. The media no longer sounds the alarm but behaves like the propaganda arm of the CCP. A few examples should suffice to prove my point.

Following the 2020 election fiasco, many on the Right refused, and still refuse, to accept the election as anything but problematic or downright stolen from the sitting President. When many conservatives sought to voice their concerns, social media, aided by the MSM, vilified them as conspiracy theorists or as dangerous to the "democratic" ways of America. China certainly was happy having aided in the removal of Trump. They now had their own "man" in the highest office of America, and they bragged about it. Now business would return to "normal" because Trump was gone, and they knew they could control Biden (note my earlier comments about Hunter Biden's laptop).

A few brave and informed politicians on the Right were not buying the new normal and began asking questions about what had happened during the 2020 election. They took to the airwaves to sound the alarm. However, the MSM would have none of the Right's so-called "propaganda" because the MSM had been in on the whole Biden-Harris scam to begin with (I would point my reader again to the now infamous *Time* article).[51] Instead, they closed ranks with the Democrat party and coerced or insisted that any lawmakers from a conservative bent who appeared on their networks must admit that the Biden administration is a "legitimate" governing administration. They badgered politicians on air to admit to the rest of America that the election was fair and free from fraud. When some refused to do so, reporters and news anchors would shut off their microphones or get up and leave the studio set. And in the post-election fracas and events of Jan 6, 2021, MSM outlets called for the silencing of any other media outlet that did not toe the line about the "perfect" election. This is totalitarianism!

A similar thing happened to those who turned to their online platforms to get the word out about election interference from China or voting anomalies that did not make sense. On most of the Big Tech sites, anyone who said anything against the supposed "fairness" of the election or who used the word "fraud" had their websites, social media pages, or Twitter accounts cancelled, blocked, or their YouTube channel banned and/or demonetized. More than one conservative pointed out that the actions of the MSM and Big Tech was equivalent to China's "disappearing" of people who disagree with the Communist Party line. "Disappearing" is China's practice of arresting and imprisoning (or killing) dissenters and then removing all evidence of a person's existence from online platforms and from public records. It is like they never existed, they simply "disappear." To be sure, Facebook, Twitter, and a host of other online platforms "disappeared" Trump and many other election integrity "naysayers." Others noted that the MSM's pressuring of conservatives to accept the election as "free of fraud" was akin to the "struggle sessions" of the Maoist revolution. During the communist revolution, young people notoriously forced older successful Chinese men and women into the public square and hung signs around their necks on which were written their supposed crime. The "criminals" were forced to recant for these stated "crimes."

The parallels are not just frightening, they are demonic in origin. The MSM praises the most radical policies of the Left and insist that these new laws and policies are supported by the vast majority of Americans. As supporting evidence, they offer "surveys" of American voters who support their conclusions. Of course, the surveys are usually bogus because of the heavy sampling of left-of-center voters or due to the fact that the surveys are worded in such a manner that they will lead the respondents to give a desired response. In a later chapter I will point out that this type of propaganda is on par with the coming times of the Antichrist takeover. America needs to wake up because we are not just dealing with a secular political issue, it is spiritual warfare and a spiritual takeover of our once-great nation.

The MSM as the "False Prophets" of the Last Days

If this is a spiritual issue, how might we view or understand what the MSM is doing to hasten the demise of our country? Lance Wallnau has rightly labelled the MSM as "false prophets," which is part of a triumvirate of false leaders in the last days. The false prophets of the media are joined by false apostles, that is, the politicians, and false teachers, who are our children's educators.[52] As I have been noting throughout this chapter, these "false prophets" are supposed to tell us the news only, but instead they have fanned the flames of dissension in our midst and have "prophesied" lies in order to bring about a desired outcome: the takeover of America by the Left. They truly have become an enemy of the people.

The overt attacks and lies began shortly before Donald Trump took office in 2017. The MSM propagated numerous lies and falsehoods in an effort to undermine the religious Right and the conservative populist movement led by Trump. They told us that America would decline under Trump. They insisted that he would start World War III. They opined that America as we know it would come to an end. They blamed conservative evangelicals for the election of Trump. They salivated at the thoughts of impeachments that would remove this menace from office. Much to their chagrin, none of their desired outcomes and "prophecies" came to pass.

These false prophets spoke much like the false prophet Hananiah in the book of Jeremiah chapter 28. Hananiah insisted that the exile of Judah would be short and that the temple vessels and those in exile would be returned to Jerusalem within two years (Jer 28:3, 6, 11). In response, Jeremiah warned Hananiah that he would be dead within one year because of his lies and attempts to lead the people astray and away from what God was really going to do with Judah, namely, send them all into exile and bring about the destruction of Jerusalem and the temple. Jeremiah was correct; Hananiah died within that same year (Jer 28:16–17). Similarly, the MSM prophesied, or as I like to say, "prophe-lied" what they wanted to see or what they thought would happen. They did not have the mind of God that is for sure; they had the mind of men and of the Enemy.

Conclusion

The point of this chapter has been to point out the dangers that can grip a country when the MSM becomes nothing more than a univocal propaganda arm of one party, a party set on the destruction of a country founded upon Judeo-Christian principles. Prior to the internet such a concern may not have been as great as it is today. When practically every American is now connected in some way to online platforms and/or rely on the internet for their "news" it is incumbent upon our news sources to be trustworthy. I did not even take the time or space to address the major problem facing American churches and Christian institutions and universities that are relying on print media of so-called evangelical publishers for the truth about conservative Christianity, interpretation of the Bible, and resources for teaching and preaching. This whole field is becoming "woke" as well. It is getting harder and harder to find established publishers that will even consider publishing any material that in some way challenges the status quo in America when it comes to sexual ethics, politics, economics, immigration, or what have you.

What will be the net result when the full force of the biased MSM controls every facet of our public discourse and information? It will be a uniparty in Washington, DC that will dictate how every part of our lives will function. This is what totalitarianism looks like.

7

The Cloudburst of
Totalitarianism: The
Silencing of America and the
Loss of Our Freedoms

You have probably experienced a cloudburst at some point in your life. When it happens it usually catches you somewhat unprepared, and you get drenched. Yet if we are honest with ourselves, we are to blame for not reacting to the signs of the gathering storm. We saw the dark skies and the gathering clouds; we felt the change in the air pressure, but we wanted to spend just a few more minutes outside doing whatever we were doing. And then, after it is too late, the clouds open up and dump rain on your picnic, your perfect wedding day, or your peaceful hike in the woods. If you have valuable items outside, or things that can get damaged by water, the results of a cloudburst can be devastating and costly. In worst case scenarios everything for which you have worked to prepare, like that perfect wedding day outside, is now ruined. It can be devastating. This happened to me once when I was building a house and I had many of my power tools out of my truck. I had to rush and get everything under cover. Fortunately, I got them protected from the rain before it was too late.

The signs in the "sky" of America when it comes to the threatening cloudburst of totalitarianism are visible for any American who is willing to pay attention. The ominous skies and threatening cloudburst of totalitarianism are upon us and threaten to burst upon us with devastating consequences. When it happens, it will be America's fault for not reacting soon enough. It will also be a part of God's judgment on America for our rejection of Him and His laws. In this chapter, I want to examine some of the signs in the metaphorical sky of America that serve as warning signs that totalitarianism is about to be the proverbial cloudburst noted above. In the next chapter my wife, Christine, will examine the Covid-19 crisis as a precursor or a test case for the rise of totalitarianism in America.

The Rise of Totalitarianism in America

The rise of totalitarian ideology in America has had both a long and a short history. In the former case, the radical Left has desired for their totalitarian policies to rule America since the 1960s. Thankfully, America was not ready for their brand of "equality" and "social justice" and rightly marginalized the radicals of the 60s. In this sense the laying of the groundwork for a totalitarian state has been over fifty years in the making. At the same time, the implementation of the Left's plan for a totalitarian state has happened in a relatively short period of time when one considers that in the short span of eight years of the Obama administration, the most anti-Christian president in our history, Obama wreaked havoc on practically every institution that once stood for American exceptionalism and the American way, especially when it comes to our Judeo-Christian heritage. The Democrat-controlled congress passed Obamacare which gave the state control of a large swath (one sixth) of the American economy. The radicals appointed by Obama at every level of the government and judicial branch passed or "legislated from the bench" laws attacking freedom of religion and conscience as well as societal norms that had been in place since the founding of America (gay-marriage and pro-LGBTQ legislation are just a couple examples). Author and commentator, David Horowitz has documented this rapid shift in his book *Dark Agenda*.[53] Horowitz rightly notes that many of Obama's and the Democrats' policies smack of totalitarianism and continue to threaten a civil and peaceful society. The presidency of Donald J. Trump began the process of unravelling the chaos and totalitarianism ensconced in bureaucratic policies and the status quo along with the reams of "red tape." In all fairness though, President Trump did not grasp the true totalitarian dangers of the deep state. Despite this oversight, Trump was still a major threat to the progressives for his "outside-of-the-box" approach and his "America-first" policies. What the Left had successfully achieved with lightning speed in Obama's eight years was beginning to fade in the few short years of the Trump administration. It is clear to see why the Left fought so hard, and continues to do so, to make sure Trump never saw, or ever sees again, the inside of the White House. Of course, this factor alone serves as motive for election fraud at the most egregious of levels, lest we forget the late-night "counting" spree favoring Biden in Michigan, Wisconsin, and Georgia. In the latter case it was caught on video!

The four years of Trump's rolling back of the Obama totalitarian tide was a mere bump in the proverbial highway that the deep state waited out until the Democrats regained the White House and Congress. That is why within a few days of the Biden-Harris administration taking power the hastily passed flurry of executive orders clearly showed that the Left and the deep state had had these orders ready to go once the election of Biden was "secured." Election integrity is a must for a democratic republic to stand and what the Left did in the 2020 election was nothing short of a coup. It is for this reason that the rise of radical and militant totalitarianism in America is assured unless God intervenes. Some may say it is too late, that judgment has already begun; I am not sure I would disagree with them. What the Left has done to America is nothing less than the creation of a "perfect storm," which will bring about the complete overthrow of America and its traditional values (see my concluding chapter). Judgment can come upon a people who refuse to listen to what the Bible says and who insist that their own desires come before God's plan. Sometimes, God will give a nation exactly what they want, namely, abusive government and rulers. The Bible is replete with examples of this very thing.

In 1 Samuel 8 (ca. 1050 BC) the nation of Israel insisted on having a king to rule over them. The prophet Samuel offered a stern warning to Israel related to the repercussions of their request. He quickly pointed out that having a monarchy like the nations would mean that Israel would lose their freedoms. The people insisted on having a king just the same. By the time Solomon's reign came to an end in 930 BC, every one of Samuel's warnings had come to pass. Absolute power, apart from God, corrupts absolutely. Solomon had turned into a tyrant of sorts with his bloating of the central government (1 Kgs 4:7; 10:24–29); his ceding of land in Israel to a foreign nation (1 Kgs 9:11), his paranoia about contenders for the throne (1 Kgs 11:40), and his heavy taxation policies (1 Kgs 12:4). Samuel's message was clarion, freedom comes with limited government that rules with a fear of God. This type of limited government was exactly what the founding fathers instituted in the founding of America. To be sure, Abraham Lincoln captured the heart of the founding fathers' endeavor at the Gettysburg Address on November 19, 1863, when he noted that America was supposed to have a "government of the people, by the people, and for the people."

The Silencing of the People

Already you might be saying that there are millions of Americans who are standing for limited government and freedom and that the true American "patriots" will win the day. The problem with this line of thinking, although perhaps true, is the MSM's and Big Tech's ability to silence we the People so unification cannot happen. To be sure, we are being silenced, especially when it comes to issues of morality, the exposing of election integrity and political corruption from the Left, legitimate concerns on immigration and public health policy, and the like. The Left's ability to keep the majority of conservatives silenced and marginalized through censorship is a key part of their plan to destroy America's founding principles. The Left has been working over-time since the days of Obama to make sure that any speech with which they do not agree is deemed "hateful" and to be shunned, silenced, and outlawed.[54] Now, the Biden administration is teaming up with Big Tech and asking them to censor any speech they deem as either "misinforma-tion" or "disinformation." They insist that this only relates to medical "disinformation," but rest assured this is only a ruse and any political speech they deem "offensive" or with which they disagree will soon be labeled "disinformation." In this case, our First Amendment right of "free speech" only applies to speech with which the Left agrees. In Feb-ruary of 2022, America had a front-row seat of what this can look like when Canada's Prime Minister, Justin Trudeau, enacted the Emergency Act to silence those who had a political view he deemed unacceptable or "unCanadian." Who would have ever guessed this could happen in a western democracy, yet it did. The scary part of all this is that now law students at prestigious schools across America, that is, the people who will become our judges in the future, are almost universally against free speech and seek to quash it at every turn.[55] This will bring devastation to our country in the coming years.

We witnessed the silencing of free speech during the 2020 election when the MSM, social media, and print media fell into lockstep with the Democrats and suppressed any story or opinion that challenged or contradicted their party line. The recent Facebook "whistleblower" is a fine example of the lengths to which they went and want to go. This leftist "whistleblower," who worked in the "fact-checking"/"community standards" (code for censorship) department at Facebook, was respon-sible for quashing the Hunter Biden laptop story prior to the 2020 election and now she is insisting that Facebook is not doing enough to silence dissenting voices post-election. Within days this "whistle-blower" went from primetime interviews to the floors of Congress with her "concerns." This smacks of an organized plan to push an agenda. If the Left has its way, they will complete the establishment of a totalitarian state in America through the suppression of the truth and through governmental coercion. They have already politicized and weaponized the most powerful of the federal agencies: the FBI, CIA, IRS, NSA, OSHA etc. These have been, and will continue to be, used by the Left to silence dissenters and impose their totalitarian will on the American people. A good example of this was Obama's use of the IRS under the leadership of Lois Lerner to punish his conservative enemies. This was followed by the media's refusal to cover the scandal, which of course Obama had fully expected would happen. And who can forget the spying undertaken by the FBI on the Trump campaign which led to the bogus two-year Mueller investigation. Recently it was revealed that the NSA (National Security Agency) is spying on conservative journalists and pundits.[56] The Biden regime has also empowered OSHA to go after 84 million Americans with a forced vaccination mandate. Fortunately, SCOTUS struck down this governmental overreach for private businesses, but not for healthcare workers. We also have the Biden DOJ under Merrick Garland using the FBI to target mothers and fathers who speak out at schoolboard meetings. These patriots are being labeled "domestic terrorists." Add to this mix the fact that the Biden administration wants Americans to spy on their friends and loved ones and report them to the government if they think they might be "domestic terrorists" or "extremists." Keep in mind that this is not terrorism or extremism related to radical Islam or some other tangible external or internal threat but rather it is anyone who disagrees with the Biden administration or who is adamantly opposed to how Biden gained the office of the presidency.[57] And social media platforms like Facebook are sending out warnings about "extremism" and encouraging users to report their friends and family members to the authorities. Again, remember that this "extremism" is any political speech that the Left deems undesirable or threatening to their agenda. Parents speaking out at schoolboard meetings threaten the powerful teachers' unions which are sympatico with the Democrat party and their plan to indoctrinate our children with critical race theory, sexual perversion, and anti-American propaganda. This should frighten Americans, but it seems to pass by most Americans with a mere sigh or shrug as a response. It appears that most simply do not realize or care that this is the path to a nation's downfall and destruction. It smacks of the tactics of Nazi Germany, communist Russia, and the CCP.

The Rise of the "Cancel-culture"

Another way Americans are being silenced is through the ever-present "cancel culture" mentality. Since the writing of my last book on *The Bible, Sexuality, and Culture*, the cultural upheaval has continued to manifest itself and the threats of being "cancelled" for unpopular opinions have only increased. Truly we are living in an Isaiah 5:20 world where good is called evil and evil is called good. This is evident when Cardi B's sexually explicit song, "WAP," is voted song of the year while several of Dr. Seuss's books are "canceled" because of their "offensive" nature. This is more than just ironic, it is telling of the spiritual sickness and decay of our culture, and in particular the spiritual depravity of America. This will certainly not be allowed to carry on with impunity. God is not mocked. Whatever a nation sows, that they will also reap (Gal 6:7).

Cancel culture is also attacking authors who say or do anything that goes against the woke culture or accepted political positions. Simon and Schuster's cancellation of their contract with Missouri senator Josh Hawley for his book *The Tyranny of Big Tech* (2021) simply because he challenged the 2020 election results on the Senate floor is a fine example of the cancel culture where the Left attacks political opponents. Even though it was picked up by another publisher, the fact that Hawley's book was dropped at all is troubling. Also, people who publish books challenging the current trends in our morality or sexual ethics are being threatened to have their books banned or burned in public. The book *Irreversible Damage* (2021) by Abigail Shrier challenging the appropriateness of the trans movement's undue influence on young women is a case in point. When I was researching my last book, I found out that one of the most detailed book-length treatments of the dangers of homosexuality from a medical perspective was banned from Amazon simply because of the data it presented. Amazon also banned Ryan Anderson's book *When Harry Became Sally* (2018) dealing with issues related to transsexuality. We as a nation are approaching a dangerous place where we follow the orders and dictates of a corrupt governing class with blind obedience because, they say, we need to "follow the science." This smacks of a similar path down which many Germans went during WWII.[58] Such actions are not only totalitarian in nature they are one more step towards full-blown fascism.

Fascist tactics are now being employed regularly by the Left's "shock troops." Despite the denials of the liberal elites, BLM and Antifa are the de facto "brown shirts" of the Democrat party. When called upon, they rove the streets of Democrat controlled cities at will spreading terror. While many examples could be offered, I will give one example. Over the July 4th weekend of 2021, a lady who was in a Los Angeles spa filed a complaint with the owner when she saw a trans man-to-woman client parading around the women's section of the spa with their male genitalia exposed to both the women and a young girl. When others joined in a peaceful protest, the next day, Antifa thugs showed up and not only threatened the peaceful protesters, but they chased and beat them because, according to Antifa, they were "transphobes."[59] The police were nowhere to be found.

Totalitarianism within Government Agencies and Social Justice Movements

I could easily use an entire book to address the way the governing class of America has adopted totalitarian tactics with our full consent because of who we elect and because we do not hold them accountable. A few examples should suffice to prove my point that we are quickly coming to the place of God's judgment by allowing our political decisions to lead to our own demise. First, a visible example of totalitarianism at the national level was on full display when our capital became an armed "green zone" after the over-hyped "riots" of January 6, 2021. For months our capital was fenced in as the political elites supposedly feared for their lives from "insurrectionists" and the "deplorables." And for those unfortunate enough to have entered the capital building, over a year later they are still being held in jail in harsh conditions as "domestic terrorists." Now we are finding out that the FBI may have instigated or at least known about the supposed riot,[60] but had planned all along to use the January 6th event to make examples of those who participated in the "riot" in order to send a message to the "deplorables" that anyone who tried to protest Biden's presidency on January 20, 2021 (or later), would be targeted and their lives destroyed for the most minor of offences. This is tantamount to these people being nothing more than political prisoners, a reality common in communist countries. This should frighten every American when the government can target people simply for minor offenses. You can decide for yourself whether the events of January 6th merited the harsh reaction of our government but what is clear is that our nation is becoming increasingly divided between the ruling class and the "un-washed" masses. This reflects the warning of Jesus himself when he said a nation divided against itself will not stand.

Second, in July of 2021, Democrat Speaker of the House, Nancy Pelosi, issued orders to open satellite field offices in Florida and California for the DC capital police.[61] Why would the "capital" police need to be outside of DC? We have the FBI for any domestic security concerns that cross state lines. This is a dangerous precedent and a first step in the nationalization of our police force. Police states always follow a similar trajectory.

Third, both of our national political parties have done nothing to address the issue of our national debt, which is at an all-time high. Even now, Congress is pushing the debt ceiling higher and higher with support from both parties while inflation is on the increase. We cannot sustain this. Such recklessness can only be explained by the fact that the Left wants to collapse our system so they can remake it as a socialistic and totalitarian state. This is what I classify as a "natural" judgment simply because we do not hold our politicians accountable and because we take money from the government that we did not earn. I am not speaking about taxpayer funded social programs like unemployment insurance or social security payments. I am speaking of government bailouts, pork-barrel spending, union kickbacks and the like.

Fourth, tax-and-spend policies that lead to nothing more than government redistribution of wealth is a means of bringing our country to the brink of not just financial ruin, but socialistic and communistic rule. On this latter point, allow me to expand. For the past few years since the rise of the likes of AOC, Cori Bush, Rashida Tlaib, Ilhan Omar, and others of their ilk within the Democrat party, we have witnessed a push for all-out socialism and totalitarian control of the American people. All of us by now are familiar with the infamous Green New Deal, which is a blueprint for a totalitarian takeover of all aspects of our country. You may be thinking that this would never happen in America, but I would warn otherwise. The reality is many in the Democratic party are not just socialistic in their leaning, several are directly connected to the Communist Party of America. This is why the Left has such a cozy relationship with China. They are trying to bring down America from within and pave the way for a globalist utopia. The problem with this global utopia is that China will be on the top of the heap calling the shots.

Another disturbing trend is the marriage of the socialistic and communistic ideology of the Left with their push for what is known as "social justice." I will begin by offering a warning to Christians who are caught up in social justice issues. This is the Left's code phraseology for redistributive justice at the state level, that is, communism.[62] Even former Chinese citizens who grew up in Maoist China and who now live in America are calling out what schools are teaching and the division they are sowing as being the same as what they experienced growing up in communist China.[63] Social justice is not "helping the poor" as many duped Christians think, it is the forced confiscation of private property for the purpose of redistribution to those who are the "have nots" in order to promote the Left's brand of "equity." We must remember that when the Left uses the term "equity" it does not mean equality. Equal opportunity is good and right but equity demands equal outcomes which is impossible apart from state coercion. Of course, this is at the heart of problematic movements associated with social justice like the LGBTQ movement, racial justice, the BLM movement, and the list goes on.[64] Therefore, social justice as defined by American academic elites is not Christian. It is not something Christians should embrace. We need to help those in need; the Bible requires this. But we must run away from what is being peddled in our universities (and some churches) today.

The Left's push for social justice is also devoid of God. They think that they have the answers to bring about equity, equality, and justice for the oppressed when they themselves are deeply flawed by sin. Due to this flaw, they will ultimately destroy everything and every life they come into contact with by their failed ideology rooted in unforgiveness and hate.[65] I am reminded of the irony of the actions of one of the founders of BLM who took the money intended for the poor and downtrodden within the African American community and went on a buying spree purchasing several homes in ritzy and predominantly White neighborhoods. While I certainly would never begrudge a person buying a home with money duly earned, I find it disingenuous that someone would give themselves a fat paycheck for "helping" the underclass and then spend it on themselves. Once again, the vital flaw of this ideology is the failure of people to recognize the fallenness of the human condition and the evil inherent in the human heart due to original sin.

When Christians embrace such problematic theories, they are supporting the very ideology that despises the Christian message. In this regard, social commentator, David Horowitz, rightly notes that "The social redeemers view the Christian concern for the salvation of individual souls as counterrevolutionary, a *cause* of social oppression. To them religious believers are obstacles on the path to the future— and must be removed. That is why progressives have declared war on religious liberty, which is America's founding principle. And that is why they seek to silence and suppress its defenders."[66] Believers who align themselves with these social movements do not realize that they themselves will become the focus of the racists sooner than later. Their faith and hope in a Savior who saves from personal sins is a direct affront to those who reject God and in turn reject original sin. For the radical Left, "sin" is a collective issue that is to be laid at the feet of their "oppressors." That is why minorities in these groups insist that they cannot be racist because they are the "oppressed." What they fail to realize is that their own sin has blinded them to the reality that they need a Savior. Salvation for them and their cause can never come from personal attainment no matter how hard they seek it. The issue of the fallenness of humanity will always get in the way. Their answer is to have the state force their ideology upon the populace. As I noted above, greed, envy, jealousy, malice, pride, and any of the other seven deadly sins, will lead them to turn on themselves and fail in their attempts at utopia. That is why communism always ends in disaster. This has not stopped the Enemy though in his attempt to destroy our nation. Our refusal to push back *en mass* against this flawed and demonic ideology is, I believe, part of the delusion that is gripping our nation, a delusion that God will use to judge America (2 Thess 2:11). This is made evident in our willingness to allow the radicals to educate our children.

The Indoctrination of Our Children

In keeping with the topic I introduced above, I want to highlight the juggernaut that we are facing as a nation in the educational institutions of our country. This week as I was writing this chapter, I read a headline related to the problematic issue of critical race theory (CRT). Even though several states (twenty as of last count) are outlawing the teaching of this divisive theory, more than 5000 teachers have signed a pledge to teach the theory regardless of the laws prohibiting it.[67] This was followed by one of America's largest teachers' unions defiantly declaring that they will not only continue to teach CRT in all 50 states and 14,000 school districts but they will also legally defend those who defy the law because they will not be silenced in teaching "the truth" about America's history.[68] Such lawless audacity and duplicity is only rivaled by perhaps the CCP. The CCP has done the same thing when teaching the "truth" of their history as well as US interaction with China, the latter of which is nothing but blatant falsehoods told to create a narrative supported by the CCP. For example, today in China even graduate students do not know the truth about the horrors that the CCP has perpetrated against its own people, nor do they know about America's efforts to aid in the development of their country.[69] And here we are allowing the Marxists do the same thing with our children through the 1619 project and CRT.

For those unfamiliar with CRT, CRT seeks to interpret history and current culture through the lens of race and power. Those who support CRT also strive to teach children that we are a systemically racist country that has consistently marginalized those in our midst who are not White. It is a means of indoctrinating our children not only to hate America and the principles upon which the nation was founded, but it also teaches that being White (a fact that people cannot change) is somehow shameful. Put simply, it is an attempt to reject our Judeo-Christian principles and our Constitution along with how people are created by God. What ever happened to the call of Martin Luther King Jr. who said he dreamed of a day when people would not be judged by the color of their skin but by the content of their character?

We need to denounce these movements for what they are; racist and divisive. Christians must declare Paul's words in Galatians 3:28 that "There is neither Jew nor Greek, there is neither slave nor free man, there is neither male nor female; for you are all one in Christ Jesus" (NASB). God needs to be the center of all we do, not race, gender, or sexual proclivities. Yet the Left has perpetuated the lies that people should be judged based upon the color of their skin, their sexual proclivities, their economic status and the like. This radical trend did not begin a few years ago, this has been going on for some time now. In fact, Horowitz is certainly correct to note that the divisive SCOTUS decisions related to abortion, social and cultural issues, and religious liberty have been the catalyst for polarizing the nation.[70] Now, Black racist organizations are declaring all-out war on anyone who is White. I read a headline recently that was downright frightening. It said, "National Black Power

Convention Activist says a time to 'kill everything white in sight' will soon come."[71] This is what is at the heart of CRT and the BLM movement both of which are being propagated to our children in classrooms across America. Unfortunately, it is also being peddled in our churches through self-professing "Christians," who hate their White brothers and sisters. In this regard, I read about an African American woman who wrote in a supposed "prayer" book for the Church asking God to help her "hate" white people.[72] With such division and hatred being spread now even in the Church, is there any wonder why I and my wife have been arguing throughout this book that America is under judgment? Our nation and our institutions, education especially, are corrupt from top to bottom and our children are on the receiving end of the hate being spewed. The result has been an entire generation that now hates or are "ashamed" of their country.[73] Instead of the founding principles of liberty and freedom, they seek a socialistic utopia. Totalitarianism is indeed upon us. We are witnessing the demise of America, a fitting judgment for our complete rejection of God.

Conclusion

There are certainly several responses one could give to the warnings I have noted above concerning what is quickly coming upon America. Totalitarianism may not take complete control of America this year or next, but it is still very much present in our political, media, entertainment, and educational systems and institutions. Some have argued that the divisions in our nation will ultimately lead to civil war. California pastor, Jack Hibbs, notes that civil war is coming because Biden's administration will kill the first and second amendments. He goes on to note that the Constitution died, or at least was "fatally shot" prior to Biden's arrival on the scene as "president" and has been bleeding out dying a slow death: Biden will complete the death.[74] While I am in agreement with Hibbs's assessment to a degree, I feel we have been in a cold civil war for decades now. Whether this will turn into a literal civil war between the Left and the Right based upon ideological beliefs and desires to control the trajectory of America, or whether it is more of a spiritual civil war remains to be seen. But mark my words, a war is coming and is already here. And the Church is going to be in the middle of it whether we like it or not. The totalitarian state is on a collision course with the true Church, and it is even now preparing the hearts and minds of the "useful idiots" to wage this war. In our next chapter my wife, Christine, gives a sobering example of just how easy it is for the Enemy to brainwash the masses into accepting totalitarianism and in turn to reject our freedoms given to us by God. Of course, this is just another step towards America turning our backs on God Himself.

8

The Calm Before the Storm: The Covid Crisis as a Precursor to the Rise of the Totalitarian State

Most people have experienced the literal calm before a storm. It is the time just prior to a major storm when you know what is coming. The air pressure drops; the sky turns an awful shade of green; the wind changes; you know the feeling. There can also be a false sense of security, when you wonder how a beautiful day can disappear so quickly. The period of calm can dissipate rapidly and turn into a violent storm, often bringing absolute devastation in its wake. You knew it was coming. You saw the signs, and hopefully you prepared by getting to safety.

In many ways, America is experiencing a similar "calm before the storm." The storm America is facing, however, is the totalitarian state. Those who are alert to the changing "weather" of the political climate are seeing the signs that will lead the nation into a period of absolute devastation and destruction. It is perhaps one of the more troubling aspects of God's coming judgment because "we the People" of these

United States are hastening the coming judgment because of our complacency. Let me explain.

As a parent, I, Christine, try to raise my children well. I have read books about discipline in order to train my children better. Many of them suggest role playing through different scenarios to prepare children for these situations. If you are going on a flight for the first time and you are worried about your kids, many authors suggest making the layout of a plane with seats in your house and role playing what will happen on the flight. These pretend play times prepare your children to be at ease in new situations. Adults also need to be prepared and groomed to enter into new conditions. How many times do we practice what we may say in an interview, or visualize how an event may go to calm ourselves so we are ready for the actual event? As I look around today, I am convinced that in many ways we are being groomed for totalitarianism. It may not look like the old style Russian communist totalitarianism, but we are being trained, nonetheless. God's judgment, as we have been noting throughout, may come in the form of the taking away of freedoms. Totalitarian governments of the past and present, are, I would argue, a form of judgment since most outlaw or limit free expression of worship.

Preparing a freedom-loving country for totalitarianism takes time. This has certainly not happened overnight, but it would appear that the Covid pandemic escalated the plans. When Babylon attacked and defeated Judah, it did not entirely decimate it or its population initially. Instead, Nebuchadnezzar, the king of Babylon, first took some of the leading elites to Babylon. When he attacked again, he took more of the population and spread them out throughout his occupied territories. Finally, when Babylon once again exiled the people of Judah, there was not much resistance either in Judah or in the areas in which the exiles lived. They had been prepared for such an outcome by Babylon. Once in Babylon they faced an uphill battle to maintain not only their religious beliefs, but also their identity. Their way of life—how they educated their children, the way they treated health concerns, how they governed themselves—now fell under the purview of Babylon. As we see in the

Bible, many of the countries at the time were not tolerant of diversity of thought that in any way opposed or challenged the dominant ruling power. We know that when the Jews were allowed to return to Israel, not all of them went. Some had become comfortable in their new surroundings; some may have even left the faith of their forefathers for the protection of the governing state's religion. In any case, the state's control became total.

As we look around our country, we begin to see the makings of a totalitarian state. Taking away the freedoms that we know is a slow process, but we can see the process taking place, nonetheless. In many ways, Covid has been our practice run. It has started the "exile" process of leaving people without their normal defenses, and therefore they have turned to the government for answers and a way forward. With each new mandate, we have seen freedoms and liberties taken away. We have seen people shaken with fear, and for many of us, our eyes have been opened to the inching toward totalitarianism happening before our eyes.

As the name suggests, totalitarianism is a type of government in which everything is controlled by the state. In the case of Russia, this started with economic control, in Germany with racial and social control. Both lead to the same endpoint in which the government decides what is best for you in all aspects of your life, and in essence becomes god to you. In order to do this, the state must control economic functions, education, the military and the police, health, the news, and spirituality. In this chapter I will first examine how the current Covid issue has opened doors for totalitarianism in the field of health, how this has in turn spilled over into our news, our education, and finally our spirituality. Once a totalitarian regime is ensconced, we will see that our daily lives will no longer be our own, but rather dictated by the state. This is a form of judgment in that God will give us what we "want"—no longer will we be tied to a Judeo-Christian faith as the underpinnings of our society, but rather the government will become our god, rewarding those who maintain the party line and punishing those who dare to disagree.

The Health Sector: How We Relate to Our Bodies

We have begun to worship at the altar of healthcare. This seems to manifest itself in two different ways. The first is the burgeoning diet business, which rakes in an estimated 72 billion dollars a year. People want to get slimmer, more fit, and look better. Many people are trying to eat better and take care of themselves. These are all good things, as long as they do not take center stage of your life. On the other end of the scale, we have a large section of our population that does not focus on diet and exercise, but rather believes medication or even not doing anything is a better way forward. A 2019 study by Roosa Tikkanen and Melinda K. Abrams, entitled, *U.S. Health Care from a Global Perspective, 2019: Higher Spending, Worse Outcomes?*[75] compared the US with other industrialized nations. The study revealed that we ranked low on almost all markers. We spent more than other countries on healthcare, but instead of seeing a strong correlation with health, we were dying at a higher rate from preventable diseases such as diabetes. Of course, we already know that we have the highest rates of obesity. It seems that we have come under the impression that if we simply medicate ourselves, issues stemming from poor health will not affect us, but this simply is not true.

As we watched how Covid acted in patients, several things became evident. First, for those who were mainly healthy, this was a survivable disease. Second, in many people who already struggled with health issues, these issues exacerbated their Covid infection. It was as if Covid sought out and exploited the inherent weaknesses in our bodies. Those who were obese, or diabetic, seemed to have some of the greatest struggles with the disease. As I watched the unfolding of how we understood this disease it seemed that it morphed itself into what would hurt someone the most, almost on an individual basis. It was a pinpoint attack.

The physical attack, however, seemed to pale in comparison to the spiritual attack that rendered people completely susceptible to the panacea of government intervention. Faced with a previously unknown contagion, we agreed to government dictums to isolate ourselves. When the government told us to wear masks, we obliged. They told us to stay inside, so we closed our doors without even thinking twice. We thought only the worst of those who would dare go somewhere without a mask. How selfish! How ignorant! We were told this was our patriotic duty. We were told that this was a kindness shown to others, all the while the MSM and government agencies fed us with a healthy dose of fear. Fear of the virus, and fear of each other lest we forget Project Veritas's undercover video of CNN's plan to do just that.[76] As I watched, (and continue to do so) all I could see was a strong spirit of fear descend on our country. That was the true virus, and it did its work masterfully.

Fear seeks to isolate people. I do not watch horror films, but I know enough that in a horror movie when one person is left alone or decides to go down a dark hallway by himself, he is not long for the film. Fear picks us off one by one, and this is what has happened during the Covid pandemic. It has worn down our immunity to the emotion of fear by keeping us inside and away from others. Now people, in the grips of fear and anxiety, are dying faster from Covid than those who are of a sound mind.[77] I am reminded of the warning of Jesus that in the last days people's hearts will fail them for fear (Luke 21:26). In Hannah Arendt's seminal work, *The Origins of Totalitarianism*, she concludes that the precursors to totalitarianism are isolation and loneliness. In fact, these things are what prepares people for totalitarianism.[78] Isolation tells people that they are impotent to do or change anything, and loneliness tells people they have no true relationships. Terror invades their lives in all aspects, and they cannot escape, therefore the illusion of safety and control from the state looms large. What has been so insidious about this round of Covid fear is that we have been told to stay isolated to make a difference. It has only weakened us more.

Now the government has offered the cure—the "vaccine"—and we should all sign up for our "medicine." I have never seen a drug disseminated at such a rate as this gene therapy has been. Let us be clear, this is an experimental drug, and we are treating it like aspirin. Everyday people post their vaccine pictures on Facebook as a means to encourage others to get it too. I remember what this kind of action used to be called: peer pressure, and we were all told to flee from it.

We have been groomed for years to think that vaccines are the one thing that truly protect us from diseases. I remember when I was pregnant with one of my kids and the zika virus was making the headlines. It was thought to have caused babies to be born with small heads. Each news segment about it ended with the phrase, and there is "no vaccine for the zika virus." As a parent today I am bombarded with the pressure to vaccinate my children as infants. The day after they are born, infants are now often immunized against hepatitis B, a disease spread through unprotected sex and sharing needles. Why are we inoculating infants against this? The list of immunizations continues, some of which are supposed to prevent treatable diseases. In other words, if your child does happen to catch some of these diseases, of course, not all of them, he or she can be treated with antibiotics or antitoxins. Yet parents are pushed by fear to give these to children so that we are "safe." If nothing else, I think Covid has taught us we are not safe.

What is even more alarming is how this drug therapy is being incentivized. The CDC has recently changed its recommendations that if you are part of the drug trial, you no longer need to wear a mask inside. As soon as this changed, stores followed suit. Recently, I walked into the grocery store which had a sign stating, "if you are vaccinated you may shop unmasked, otherwise you must be masked." States and cities have offered prizes for those who choose to enter the drug trial. In essence, life can go back to normal if you only bow to the State's understanding of what is best for you. Follow their guidelines and you will be safe. No longer is our trust in God, but in our healthcare system. It makes me think of Ben Franklin's famous maxim: "Those who would give up essential Liberty, to purchase a little temporary Safety, deserve neither Liberty nor Safety." The irony in trusting government over God is that the former is notoriously fallible. Since those early months of the push to vaccinate everyone, the rules have changed multiple times. We are now being told that everyone must again mask up and social distance no matter what your vaccine status.

Sometimes God gives us what we think we want. In the books of Exodus and Numbers, the Israelites grew tired of manna, they wanted some meat to stick to their ribs. God's good gift of sustenance was not enough, it was monotonous. I think some may have feared they were missing out on the good things of life and the good food they left behind. In response to their complaints, God gave them quail, so much that they got physically sick of it (Num 11:18–20). There is nothing wrong with quail. And there is nothing inherently wrong with medicine or vaccines. However, when they become what you put your trust in instead of God, then we have a problem. I am not condemning everyone who has received a vaccine. I am merely pointing out the question: what is driving this rush toward it? The answer is fear. We think we know what is best and we rush headlong into a possible solution without assessing all the risks. We long for safety, but it is only in God that we are truly safe. When I look around and see the effects of Covid on our bodies and how we understand our bodies, I see the judgment of God calling us back to Himself.

The News and Media: How We Relate to Others

There is an old adage that says, "You are what you eat." Many people have revised this to "You are what you think." What are we consuming as a culture, and who is offering this diet? I would simply respond, fear and the lies of the MSM respectively. In George Orwell's *1984*, Winston Smith's occupation is to re-write history. Every day he is given things to correct in the newspaper archive so that the current Party line is viewed with perfect historical accuracy. Often this means fabricating either production goals or production amounts, or both. For example, he muses on the chocolate rations: "It appeared that there had even been demonstrations to thank Big Brother for raising the chocolate ration to twenty grammes a week. And only yesterday, he reflected, it had been announced that the ration was to be REDUCED to twenty grammes a week." The Party dictated what the people believed. While we may not yet be living under the "Party," we have been living under a Big Tech and Media oligarchy for information, and any deviation is met with disdain and cancelation. When we are not allowed to think or engage in debate, I believe this is a signaling of totalitarianism, and therefore judgment.

This phenomenon—the changing of history before our eyes—is occurring today. Perhaps the most striking example was during the SCOTUS confirmation hearings of Amy Coney Barrett. When asked about her views on discrimination based upon one's sexuality, she said that she would never discriminate based upon "sexual preference." Within a few hours, Judge Barrett was lectured about how the phrase "sexual preference" was an outdated term, it was derogatory, and unacceptable to be used. Judge Barrett was clearly baffled by this, but apologized. In fact, sexual preference had been an acceptable term up until *she*, a conservative woman, used it. Merriam-Webster changed its online dictionary entry about it that day to state that sexual preference was offensive. A few months previously Joe Biden had used the term with impunity. Now, to be fair, there is a 2013 Slate article by Jesse Bering entitled, "Stop Saying 'Sexual Preference': You May Mean Well, But It Makes You Sound Ignorant," in which he calls for the phrase "sexual orientation" to be used instead.[79] However, this clearly did not catch on. What we witnessed in this example was what Orwell predicted: the censoring of the past to control the present. In the course of a few hours a term became offensive and derogatory. This is a step closer to totalitarianism. It does not allow for people to have opposing viewpoints.

As we closed our doors to the outside world during the Covid crisis, the MSM and online social media programs became more important. We depended on them not only for news of the world but also of each other. Unable to meet face to face, we needed some way to ward off the loneliness and fear. Many hailed programs such as Zoom and Facebook as an antidote for loneliness and remaining in contact with each other. The problem is we know that these programs, instead of bringing people together, can actually keep people apart.

Before the Covid pandemic, we were already dealing with the effects of increased social media use. As more people purchased smart phones, which "connect" us with more people, the rates of depression and suicide climbed ever upward.[80] As we turn to our phones for meaningful connection, we actually decrease our relational ties. A University of Pennsylvania study found "that when students decrease their social media use below 30 minutes a day, they have a significant improvement in their well-being."[81] By minimizing our time online and maximizing our time in person, we decrease depression, we decrease loneliness, and we increase our happiness. In the pandemic, by shutting ourselves in and only relying on the already problematic modes of social media and virtual communication, we set ourselves up for increased levels of loneliness. A Harvard University Loneliness in America Report estimated that 36 percent of Americans experienced loneliness during the pandemic, and 61 percent of those were between 18 and 25.[82]

Loneliness leaves us vulnerable to both physical and spiritual attack. Loneliness suppresses the body's immune system and makes it harder to get well. In fact, "Loneliness has been implicated in everything from increased risk of hypertension and heart disease to a reduced antibody response to the flu vaccine."[83] Our bodies get worn down from it. We all know that when we do not feel well physically, it can be hard to feel well spiritually and emotionally. The Enemy uses loneliness and fear to tell lies. When we sin, we fear confessing our faults lest people leave us once they see the depth of our depravity. Loneliness and depression tell us that no one will want to be our friend because of our faults. Therefore, we no longer rely on people, and are forced to rely on the virtual world to gain our meaning and our information. As we have witnessed, the MSM is in the business of fear mongering, which will only divide and exacerbate feelings of loneliness, leaving us vulnerable to a totalitarian regime.

Religion: How We Relate to God

In the early centuries of Christianity, plagues ravaged Rome. The natural response was to flee Rome and stay as far away from people as possible. The early Christians, however, with an eye on the everlasting hope we have in Jesus, bucked the normal reaction and ran toward the plague and its victims. Cyprian writes:

> By the terrors of mortality and of the times, lukewarm men are heartened, the listless nerved, the sluggish awakened; deserters are compelled to return; heathens brought to believe; the congregation of established believers is called to rest; fresh and numerous champions are banded in heartier strength for the conflict, and having come into warfare in the season of death, will fight without fear of death, when the battle comes.[84]

Their example of heavenly focus inspired others to become Christians. By their actions they illustrated the power of the true God, and by contrast, they showed the impotence of Rome's emperors in the face of natural disaster.

The Church as God's representative on earth has a responsibility to offer to an unbelieving world evidence of why they should believe. Christians have done this, and many continue to do so, but on the whole, the Church has ceded its responsibilities to the State and other organizations. When faced with this pandemic, many Christians, myself included, followed what the government dictated: stay at home, and stay away from people. While our forebears rushed to the site of pain and suffering, we sheltered in place. This is not to say that some Christians did not help. I know some churches offered food relief, for example. But for the most part, we have left the ministry of presence and healing to the "medical professionals." Gone are the days that Christians ran hospitals, now they are run by secular conglomerates with a suspicious eye to what Christians can offer. One need only remember how Franklin Graham's attempt to aid New York City during the early Covid scare through his charitable organization, *Samaritan's Purse*, was viewed in a suspect manner.

This is also the case with education. The original Sunday Schools were schools geared toward children who worked in factories and could not go to school. These were ministries of the Church to teach children to read and do basic math. Many early church schools offered low or no cost education to many children. In some areas they offered the only available education for students. Now the public schools dominate the field of education and offer no spiritual solace. In the areas of healthcare and education, the Church has ceded this ground, and will not be able to reclaim it. These were two areas in which we could act as a light to a dark world.

Now we are on the verge of ceding even our ground of worship. As Covid shut down houses of worship, most scrambled to offer some sort of ministry to the faithful. In many cases, this meant streaming lonesome worship services with only a few members of the clergy or worship team, praising God to an empty worship space. Some churches, such as ours, offered drive-in services, to at least give the semblance of meeting together. Small groups were relegated to the ubiquitous zoom call, which does not really engender community, but rather a second-rate virtual one.

The pandemic has highlighted the cracks in the Church. In August of 2020, David Kinnamen of the Barna Group estimated that one in five churches will close permanently primarily because of a drop in tithing.[85] In an NPR interview, Kinnamen outlined that even though some churches had started opening up, many churches saw smaller numbers of people attending. In fact, in July 2020, the Barna Group found that roughly 1 in 3 Christians had stopped attending church. In the face of severe hardship, the Church is called to offer solace and sustenance, yet it seems we are simply trying to survive ourselves. By moving away from in-person worship and relying on the cold virtual world of streaming worship, we are only adding to the loneliness many people have experienced.

Finally, some churches were already dying before the Covid pandemic. A 2019 study for the Anglican Church of Canada by the Rev. Dr. Neil Elliot, PhD, found that by 2040 the Anglican Church of Canada will have no parishioners. This was based on a steady sixty-year trend. Elliot writes: "There is no sign of any stabilisation in our numbers; if anything the decline is increasing. Some had hoped that our decline had bottomed out, or that programs had been effective in reversing the trends. This is now demonstrably not the case."[86] The Church is losing its voice and its members slowly, but surely. And yet, they are willing to cede more ground. Soon after the pandemic hit, most of the Anglican bishops and clergy wrote a letter to the government of Canada pleading that this was the time to consider guaranteed income for all Canadian citizens. Instead of stepping up to offer comfort in the face of adversity, the Church hurried to look to the government for help, which will ultimately lead to totalitarian control.

Conclusion

If the past couple of years are any indication of how the Church as a whole will fare during hard times, then we are woefully unprepared. And I am sick and tired of hearing, "The Church needs to be the Church." Yes, we do, but that leads to so little action. So, I will leave you with a few ideas about how to move forward. Totalitarianism is knocking at our door, and we are just staring at it, hoping it will simply go away.

If we desire truly to be the Church, we need to invest our time with each other. While the internet was helpful as a stopgap in the time of Covid, we must not rely on it as the sole method of fellowship. In-person gatherings, both big and small need to occur. This is how true relationships are formed. We need to re-humanize our interactions with each other, away from technology, or else we will see technology as our savior, which it is not. We need to get serious about prayer, fasting, and encouraging each other. Ask yourselves if God has positioned your church family in a way to take back the ground that the Church has ceded to government. How can you provide for education, health care, the poor, and the needy? God may be calling your church to a new ministry.

Invest time with your family. Read aloud different books, not only the Bible, but also books about different missionaries or other wholesome literature. Prepare yourselves by rehearsing how God has moved in the past. Teach your children about propaganda. Give them tools to discern what is good and true and right. And most of all, warn them of the dangers of rejecting God, an action that will have devastating consequences for both the individual, and the nation.

Finally, I want to conclude with a final thought that has come to me as I have written this chapter. As I think of the need for safety, the Lord has reminded me of part of a prayer from the Anglican tradition known as "Evening Prayer," which I prayed every day during seminary: "Give peace, O Lord, in all the world; for only in You can we live in safety." There is only one true safe place in the world—in the hands of the Father.

9

Rejecting Our "Chief Meteorologist": God in the Hands of Angry Sinners

A meteorologist is one who reports, forecasts, or predicts coming storms by referencing and studying weather patterns both past and present based upon computer models. We trust meteorologists because they are supposed to be trained in their field and know what they are talking about. Navigators of all types (ships, planes, spacecraft) rely on meteorologists in order to have safe trips for themselves and their passengers. Now imagine what would happen if you boarded a plane with the weather looking threatening and foreboding only to find out that the pilot decided to ignore the meteorologists and fly into the eye of a storm. You would probably wait for the next flight to wherever you were traveling. I know I would. This may sound ludicrous, and of course it is, but what America has done, and is continuing to do, is exactly the same when it comes to our rejection of God and His Word. God gave us the Bible not only as a means of navigation for the country, but also for the "reports and forecast" of what is coming our way. We need our "Chief Meteorologist" to give us clear direction and warnings.

Allow me to offer a fine biblical example of this concept. As I was reading Lance Wallnau's most recent book titled *God's Chaos Code*, I was reminded of the story in the Gospels where Jesus and the disciples set sail on the Sea of Galilee to cross to the region of the Gadarenes (Luke 8:22–26). During the trip, a storm arose and threatened to swamp and sink the boat; however, Jesus was asleep in the back part of the ship. When the disciples awakened him in great distress, Jesus calmed the storm simply by saying, "Peace, be still." The disciples were dumbfounded and amazed at the miracle and by the fact that their master had the ability to calm the storm merely by speaking. When it comes to America, we need to keep in mind that when a nation rejects the Master of the wind and storms (both metaphorical and literal), whom I have labelled the "Chief Meteorologist," then we are setting ourselves up for judgment. Part of that judgment will be the realization that the storms of life and of culture are going to sink our "ship" because we have removed Jesus and God from our "boats" and attempted to navigate stormy waters without him.

In light of these metaphors and parallels, in this chapter, I want to examine briefly how America's rejection of God will, and has, hastened God's judgment on America. At all levels of society and government, the Left has systematically removed God from our nation. Without recognizing and welcoming God's direction for our country, America is doomed like so many other great nations and civilizations of the past that followed the same path. We cannot continue waging war on God, and anything related to the Christian faith, without reaping the negative consequences. Great religious leaders of the present, and the past, certainly knew this then, and know it now.

God in the Hands of Angry Sinners

For those familiar with church history in America, you will recognize that the sub-title of this chapter, "God in the Hands of Angry Sinners," is a play on the title of a well-known sermon from 18th-century America. Back in 1741, Jonathan Edwards preached a sermon titled, "Sinners in the Hands of an Angry God." When he preached the sermon to his congregation in Northampton, Massachusetts, and later at Enfield, Connecticut (originally part of Massachusetts), revival broke out. This revival fed into the First Great Awakening (ca. 1730s–1740s) in America. What made his sermon so effective was Edwards's ability to paint a vivid picture of what the judgment of God meant for those listening. America of the 18th century was in fear of being judged by a righteous and holy God. Each person sitting in the service that day recognized their complicity and their individual sinfulness before a holy God. Today, many Americans have rejected the concept of personal sinfulness and the need for repentance, especially those who have bought into Marxist ideology and liberation theory, which categorize people into the redeemable oppressed and the irredeemable oppressors. America has also collectively lost their fear of God and instead have put Him on trial and judged God to be unacceptable to our modern "American values." What will happen when we as Americans, that is, the "sinners" noted above, turn on our only Hope and reject Him outright? Again, judgment is the only thing that remains for such a nation. Just so you, my reader, may know that I am not being a sensationalist allow me to offer a disturbing array of examples of how this abandonment and rejection of God is happening in America even now.

The Removal of God from Congress

In years gone by, if one were to listen to the average politician during an election cycle you would be convinced that many of them were the most God-fearing, America-loving, flag-waving, patriotic politician to ever run for political office. While this is true in some cases even today, it has certainly been tamped down because of our rising rejection of God. Being a Christian, which used to be a favorable life choice prior to the 1990s, today is viewed as a liability. I can recall my first experiences of living in the American south and seeing politicians' campaign signage around Birmingham, Alabama, stating that politician X was a member of the local denominational church and therefore trustworthy. Coming from Canada I can remember thinking that to make these statements back home would be to commit political suicide. The experience I had was over twenty years ago. Today, most politicians hold their religious cards close to their chest. It is hard to figure out where they stand on faith and what their thoughts on Jesus, salvation, church, the Bible, and God actually are. It is usually not until after they are elected and start voting on specific legislation that the truth of who they are becomes clear for everyone to see. Now to be sure, some politicians are anti-God and anti-religion from the get-go. I am again reminded of the bold words spoken by then presidential candidate, Beto O'Rourke, when he proudly declared that he would go after any church that did not support LGBTQ issues by taking away their tax-exempt status. Other life-long politicians defiantly challenge Christian principles and God in their party platforms, through their governing, and on the floor of Congress. I will offer three examples.

First, the Democrat party has made their anti-God position readily available for all to see. They have been steadily moving in this direction and now proudly declare through resolutions that they are the party for the non-religious because the Democrat party aligns most readily with this group.[87] The pertinent part of the resolution from the 2019 Democrat platform reads, "Whereas, religiously unaffiliated Americans overwhelmingly share the Democratic Party's values, with 70% voting for Democrats in 2018, 80% supporting same-sex marriage, and 61% saying immigrants make American society stronger."[88] This says it all when it comes to what the Left stands for and the pride with which they declare their liberation from all things God. They are now a post-Christian party. And who can forget the now-famous attempt to keep language related to their affirmation of God (and Jerusalem as the capital of Israel) in their party platform in 2012 which ended with the delegates on the floor booing God![89] Of course, this makes perfect sense. The Democrat party no longer attempts to hide their rejection of God and Israel.

Second, during the Obama administration, Obama made every effort possible to marginalize Christian thought and influence from his party and administration as well as by removing any reference to God from administration-associated literature and government documents coming out of his office.[90] This has continued in Obama's "third term" now known as the Biden-Harris administration.

Finally, shortly after the Biden-Harris administration took control of the US government, one of the first bills that was proposed was the anti-Church and anti-biblical-mandates bill, HR5, conveniently disguised under the benign title "The Equality Act." While debating the bill, which will strip away the designation of male and female for people and which seeks to force Americans to pay for abortions, representative Greg Steube of Florida declared, "The gender confusion that exists in our culture today is a clear rejection of God's good design. Whenever a nation's laws no longer reflect the standards of God that nation is in rebellion against him and will inevitably bear the consequences." The congressman continued, "We are seeing the consequences of rejecting God here in our country today." In response to this plea, Congressman Jerry Nadler of NY pompously declared on the floor of Congress, "What any religious tradition describes as God's will is no concern of this Congress."[91] Can we say, step back from Mr. Nadler and allow the lightning to fall? Sadly, this is not a one off. This is the basic sentiment we have been witnessing coming from the halls of Congress since the 1960s. Legislation marginalizing biblical principles and God is now the norm, and what legislators cannot do legislatively they rely on the unelected judicial branch to enact.

The Hubris of SCOTUS: Removing God from America

As I touched on in my book *The Bible, Sexuality, and Culture*, and as poignantly noted by David Horowitz in chapters 5 and 6 of his book titled *Dark Agenda*, one cannot speak about the topic of America's rejection of God without pointing out the devastating effects of SCOTUS's abominable and unconstitutional decisions to remove prayer and Bible reading from schools in 1962 and 1963 in their *Engel v. Vitale* and *Murray v. Curlett* rulings. Since these decisions, the misuse of the

Establishment Clause and the putative "separation of church and state" mantra has led to every iteration of discrimination against Christians, and by extension, God, that one can imagine. Children and teachers are chastised and threatened with punishments at the very mention of God or the threat of a public prayer on government-owned property. Numerous court cases have only added to the blasphemous rejection of God as creator and redeemer.[92] Now SCOTUS's reliance on the bogus "right to privacy" quip supposedly contained in the Constitution, has allowed for every conceivable abomination and deviant lifestyle to be ensconced into law and become binding on every state in the union. To be sure, the founding fathers would roll over in their graves if they could see what a few unelected-black-robed ideological miscreants on the SCOTUS have done to the spiritual state of our country. As the old adage goes, "elections have consequences" and this is a case in point as many left-leaning liberal judges have sidestepped the legislative process to force upon all Americans the whims of the few by legislating from the bench. In some cases, unconstitutional legislation has been passed by one vote. So, one person can change the entire country by a yes or a no vote! Meanwhile, self-professing Christians have sat idly by and continued to vote liberals/leftists into the highest levels of government and they in turn have removed God from every level and facet of our public discourse and institutions through the nomination of SCOTUS judges who are appointed for life with no recourse for removal short of an impeachment trial.

Make no mistake, the Left is not satisfied with mere legislation, they want to crush the opposition, that is, those of us holding to Judeo-Christian values, and remake America into a secular state in every way by removing any reference to God. Whether it be the mentioning of God in the Pledge of Allegiance, or the presence of the phrase "In God We Trust" on our money, for the Left, the Judeo-Christian God must be expunged. Ironically, the Left has found in those from the Islamic "religion" a ready ally in their fight against Judeo-Christian values. As we will see, this is an unholy alliance to remove God and Judeo-Christian ideals from America.

The Unholy Alliance of the Left and Islam

The Left has climbed "into bed" with Islam and it is not going to end well.[93] While I spend more time in my next chapter on the problem of Islam in America in relation to anti-Semitism, here I focus on Islam's push to have the Left embrace Allah as the one true god. Immediately Jeremiah 2:11 comes to mind: "Has a nation changed its gods, even though they are not gods? Yet my people have changed their glory for that which does not profit" (my translation). Of course, those who study Bible history know what happened to Judah when they tried this: God judged them, destroyed their nation, and exiled the people. Today, the Left is pushing to turn us from the God who was so integral to our founding as a nation to the god of Islam. Islam is steadily growing in America through both immigration and birthrates. The purpose of the Left's policies to open wide our borders for those from Islamic traditions is twofold. First, it gives them a ready pool of voters because immigrants and Islamic people tend to vote Democrat. Secondly, Islam and the Left have the same goal: to rid America and the world of Judeo-Christian ideology, the Christian God, and Christians in general.

Again, the Left's policies speak for themselves. The Left screams that there is no place for discrimination against Islam in America, but their policies make it clear that it is open season on Christianity.[94] Have you ever noticed that homosexual couples never attempt to take an Islamic baker or florist to court for disagreeing with their lifestyles? If left unchecked, the Left's unholy alliance with Islam will not only be the undoing of Christian America, but it will also be the undoing of the Left. Once Islam gains a large enough foothold to exert its will over the "infidels," which includes those on the Left as well as Christians on the Right, Islam will steamroll the Left as well. As I noted in my latest book, one of the ways Islam conquers a nation is through immigration, which in Arabic is called *hijrah*.[95] They immigrate to a new country, have more children than the local population, and in time take over the nation through their elevated birthrates. They couple this with what is called *muruna* ("stealth" or "flexibility") in Arabic.[96] *Muruna* basically allows for a devout Islamic person to set aside Sharia law when it is necessary, or expedient to blend with the "infidels" (code for Westerners) thereby lulling Westerners into thinking they are moderate and in alignment with western goals.[97] When they have gained the upper hand numerically (which is usually only about 10 percent of the population) and have a foothold in political power, they then revert back to strict Islam and impose Sharia law on their new country. This pattern has already been seen in England. At only 5–6 percent of the population in England, Islam is exerting disproportionate control.[98] As an example of the activism of Islamic proponents in America, Palestinian Muslim activist Linda Sarsour from New York City lobbied the government until it agreed to include two Muslim holidays (Eid al-Adha—the Festival of Sacrifice [Abraham's near sacrifice of his "only" son]; and Eid al-Fitr—marking the end of Ramadan) in the NYC school calendar![99] Keep in mind that Muslims make up only between 2–4 percent of the greater NYC metro area and yet they demanded, and were given, the ability to include Muslim holidays in their calendars.[100] In a separate incident in June of 2021 an Islamic girl, while leading the Pledge of Allegiance at a Virginia high school graduation ceremony, changed the wording of the pledge (without telling anyone) stating that America is one nation "under Allah."[101] This certainly does not sound like assimilation or the American "melting pot" of the past, or the *e pluribus unum* ("out of many one") espoused by our founding fathers as the moto of America.

The difference between Islam and Western culture, the latter of which includes Christians, is that Muslims have a long view of history. In other words, they play the waiting game, even if it takes one or two hundred years or more to reach their goal. To be sure, the Left may have a longer view politically than the Right, especially in light of what they set in motion during the 1960s, but the Left is nowhere near as patient as Islamists. You do not have to take my word for it, just look at how fast the Islamic population has increased in America over the past few decades and then compare that to their growing role in Congress. We now have vocal antisemitic Islamists seated in the

Chambers of Congress and in political positions across America. They do not have the best interests of America in mind, but rather, they seek the overthrow of America by replacing the Constitution with Sharia law. Again, a quick Google or DuckDuckGo search will reveal hours of videos from Islamists across the US telling us exactly what they have planned for America. In 1900 the Islamic population in America was basically non-existent at 0.01 percent,[102] but as of 2020, Islam accounted for 1.1 percent of the population with some putting it as high as 1.4 percent with it expected to more than double by 2050.[103] If 1.4 percent is accurate, then in one century we have seen a 140-fold increase in the Islamic population which is a 13,900 *percent* increase! I am not trying to be Islamophobic, but only to sound the alarm of what their clearly stated plan is.

I offer a recent example to show the dangers that America is facing with the willingness of the Left to allow Islamic law to override American laws. In Texas, a Collin County female District judge ruled that a Muslim American citizen had to have her divorce proceedings heard before a three-man Sharia court instead of a secular court. Her reasoning? She said the woman had signed a prenuptial agreement back in 2008 stating that she would allow any marriage disagreements to be heard by the Sharia panel.[104] The problem was the Muslim woman insisted that she was tricked into signing the prenuptial document. Despite the charge, the judge refused to accept her defense. So, here we are in 2022 with a District Court judge allowing Sharia law to override the rights of an American citizen! And this is taking place in the conservative state of Texas.

How could this happen in America? Why would God allow a foreign nation and a false religion to be a part of the judgment of America? It is because God has no problem using the vilest of nations to punish His people for their lack of faith and lack of commitment to God's Word and His ways. If you do not believe me then read the book of Habakkuk. When the prophet struggled with the waywardness of Judah and the systemic sin of the nation during the late 7th century, the prophet began praying for God's intervention. In response to his prayers, God told him He was sending the Babylonians to punish His people. Habakkuk was taken aback at the thought of a nation more corrupt and godless than Judah being used by God to judge them. God simply responded that He would use Babylon to judge Judah, and then He would use another nation (Persia) to judge Babylon. In the end God's justice would be served and His people would learn the hard way that sin has consequences.

What we are facing as a nation is nothing short of cataclysmic when it comes to our godlessness, our foreign policy, our immigration policy, and the Left's proliferation of the false premise that Islam is a "religion of peace." Former Muslims themselves state clearly it is anything but a religion of peace.[105] It is a political ideology wrapped in the guise of religion being taught to Muslim immigrants across western countries in what is known as *dawa* (i.e., "a political philosophy along with its spiritual aspects" taught in Muslim schools and mosques).[106] This is the worse type of combination. ISIS gave us a front-row seat of what can happen when "radical Islam," which is actually true Islam based upon the Quran,[107] is left unchecked. They murdered Christians wholesale and unhindered across Syria and Iraq for years under the Obama administration. Islam is not the only threat to America though. In fact, in the near future, it appears like it will play more of a minor role. The real threat in the immediate future and even now is the religion of progressivism, which is quickly unseating God from every facet of American society.

The Dangers of Progressivism

Many have noted that the Progressive Left is the new religion of our time.[108] The Left has allowed the State to take the place of Jesus as Savior while they preach a different gospel, namely, that only they can save America.[109] They purport that they are the ones who can root out the "sins" of racism, injustice, oppression of the poor and downtrodden, and that only they have the answers for the disenfranchised and helpless in our midst and at our borders.[110] Put simply, America has no need for God when the Left and their version of the State can save humanity. One need only to listen to the likes of Alexandria Ocasio-Cortez to hear the new religion being preached daily while America's youth fall in line with the "gospel" of the Left. The Leftist "preachers" have the same fervor as any Pentecostal or Southern Baptist preacher but lack the power of the Holy Spirit. Theirs is a false religion, a false gospel, and we all know what Paul had to say about those preaching a gospel other than the one we have received from him: he said, let them be *anathema*, a term designating a curse in the strongest of terms (Gal 1:8–9).

Progressives have tapped into the Zeitgeist of Western culture and the rise of the postmodern ideology gripping every facet of society. For the progressives, absolute truth does not exist; truth is relative they say.[III] Gender, sexuality, societal rules, you name it, are all subject to the whims of a given culture in a given time or place. There is no "one-size-fits-all" body of truth. Conversely, they argue that the absolutes of God's Word are restrictive and in need of either reinterpretation or complete rejection. Of course, they prefer the latter. Postmodernism has found fertile ground in our post-Christian milieu and the main-line church, and many evangelicals also have bought into the lies of the Enemy. They have adopted anti-biblical positions on culture, race, sexuality, and gender and support politicians who perpetuate the goal of removing God from society.

My wife and I have talked about this dilemma at length. How is it possible that self-professing Christians support these agendas? The truth is that God's Word is coming to pass before our eyes. Paul told Timothy that in the last days that God would send a strong delusion over people so that they would believe a lie (2 Tim 2:11). Paul is speaking to young Timothy about the coming man of lawlessness who is empowered by Satan himself. If the delusion can come upon those who are unbelieving, it can also come upon the religious elite who have rejected the Gospel in favor of a false religion that rejects God and the teaching of His Word. When this happens, which is has, judgment is assured.

Conclusion

The war on Christianity and God is not going away, it is only increasing. The progressive Left has taken over the Democrat party and is waging an all-out war against God and Judeo-Christian values in America. And as we have seen since the 2020 election, many RINO ("Republican in Name Only") Republicans share the values of the mob and the Left. The founding fathers knew that if a godless society emerged in America, the experiment they had undertaken would fail. As John Adams wrote, "We have no government armed with power capable of contending with human passions unbridled by morality and religion. Avarice, ambition, revenge, or gallantry, would break the strongest cords of our Constitution as a whale goes through a net. Our Constitution was made only for a moral and religious people. It is wholly inadequate to the government of any other."[112] Adams's warning is ominous to be sure. In fact, he sounds prophetic. We have arrived at a place where his words now are proving to be true. God will judge America for its rejection of biblical values and principles. God will judge America for the Church's refusal to stand and fight for godly values. God will judge America for its arrogance of thinking we can survive without Him. God will judge America for rejecting the Bible and the founding fathers' warnings. God will judge America for the legislation of our politicians and for the heinous decisions of SCOTUS which flout God's laws. God will judge America for rejecting God while elevating and praising a false god. God will judge America because we deserve nothing less!

10

Sowing the Wind and Reaping the Whirlwind: The Rise of Antisemitism

What is the difference between wind and whirlwind? According to Dictionary.com, a whirlwind is "a relatively small mass of air rotating rapidly around a more or less vertical axis advancing over land or sea: specific categories of whirlwind include dust devil, dust whirl, tornado, and waterspout." Wind, on the other hand, can be any disturbance in the air from a simple breeze all the way to a hurricane. We all like a good breeze on a hot summer day but when the wind turns into a whirlwind and reaches the size of the meteorological phenomenon of a tornado, we quickly realize the dangers associated with the latter. To be sure, a fierce whirlwind destroys everything in its path, sucking material into its funnel and leaving nothing but carnage.

There are many similarities between the wind and the whirlwind and the *effects* of antisemitism on a society. Antisemitism in varying degrees has been around as long as the Jewish people have existed as a nation. As evidence of this, I would encourage my reader to look at Phyllis Goldstein's book *A Convenient Hatred: The History of Anti-semitism*.[113] Biblically, the actions of the Pharaoh in Egypt are a case in point, and, as we will see, the book of Esther shows the dangers when antisemitism is allowed to fester. Like our comfort with a nice summer breeze, some people may feel that a "little bit" of antisemitism is okay, but the problem is that it can quickly grow into heinous acts, lest we forget the Holocaust. Indeed, when antisemitism becomes pervasive, it is virtually impossible to stop before massive harm and damage is done. As noted in the definition above, a whirlwind revolves around a vertical central axis and then can grow into a larger storm system. Similarly, antisemitism will grow if hatred towards Jewish people is allowed to swirl around a "central axis," that is, even a small group of people who support antisemitism and anti-Israel policies. As the anti-Semites fan the flames of hate and coalesce their power, their hatred can be directed outwards with devastating effects. This is what we are seeing happen with those from the Left. There is a very centralized and concerted effort to demonize Israel and the Jewish people. It is beginning to sweep across America as other disgruntled race-baiting groups join in the vortex of antisemitism. This, too, is setting up America for God's judgment.

The first part of the title for this chapter, "sowing the wind and reaping the whirlwind" comes from Hosea 8:7. In this context the prophet is speaking about the dangers of idolatry and rejecting God. When a nation turns from God and chooses "idols," that is, any other form of worship and focus other than God (see my previous chapter), then the "whirlwind" of God's judgment is assured. In Hosea's mind, there is no such thing as a little bit of idolatry being okay. Any idolatry is an affront to God and His covenant with Israel. I would argue that this holds true for antisemitism as well. Today, the phrase "sowing the wind and reaping the whirlwind" has become a common refrain when describing a problematic event that may start out small but will ultimately bring about exponential negative results. The rising tide of antisemitism in America definitely fits this analogy.

In this chapter I want to examine the dangerous trajectory of

America, its politicians, and some of the recent political decisions that are marginalizing Israel, and by extension, Jewish people worldwide. Whether segments of the American population want to admit it or not, the Jewish people are still God's chosen people and how we treat them is an important indicator of where we are as a society. God blesses those who bless His people, and He curses those who curse His people (Gen 12:3).

Looking back at Germany of the 1930s, many of us, I am sure, have asked the question, "How did a developed, enlightened, and predominantly 'Christian' society like Germany accept Hitler, Nazism, and the rise of antisemitism?" The answer is twofold. First, human hearts are desperately wicked (Jer 17:9) and no matter what level of "enlightenment" we may boast we have attained, evil is embedded in our moral being. We can do heinous things when we turn from God. Just look at our abortion issue. If God tarries and allows America to stand, someday we will look back on *Roe v. Wade* and wonder how we could have ever allowed ourselves to get to that point. I pray we recognize this very soon. Second, the German people allowed the latent and overt antisemitism already prevalent in their society to grow into an all-out "tornado" because they coalesced around a "central axis," namely, Hitler and Nazism. The people of Germany quickly accepted Hitler's demented rantings as reality when he vilified one race of people as being the cause of the world's ills. They never thought to turn around and look in the mirror and take responsibility for their own sin until it was too late. While I pray America will not get to this point, the rising antisemitism on the Left of American politics is not leaving me too optimistic.

America's Relationship with Israel

America has had a long history of aiding the Jewish people and supporting the rise of the Jewish state in 1948. Harry S. Truman, the 33rd president of the US, was instrumental in pushing for Israel's right to exist and for their right to the land of Israel they occupy today. Similar to my discussion in Chapter 3, he actually saw himself as a Cyrus figure.[114] Since the days of Truman, America's presidents have sided with Israel in their defense and as an ally which Israel certainly needs amidst hostile Arab neighbors. That policy remained in place until the presidency of Barack Obama. Obama sidled up to the Iranian mullahs while backstabbing Israel. By the end of Obama's tenure, the Democrat party had been overrun by leftist and Marxist ideology that at its core, rejects God and by extension, those who are God's people, whether Jew or Christian. Obama consistently gave Israel's leader Benjamin Netanyahu the cold shoulder and sought to undermine his more conservative views on how to run Israel. According to *The Washington Times*, the Obama administration actually attempted to derail Netanyahu's re-election bid in 2015 by sending American taxpayers' money to help fund the opposition.[115] Now while some, especially those on the Left, may see this as good political posturing for America, the reality was that Netanyahu's conservative policies went against Obama's worldview. Obama's policies also appear to have been rooted in latent antisemitism in the Democrat party that was beginning to fester at that time.

When Donald Trump won the 2016 election the rising antisemitism within the government was tamped down by Trump's strong pro-Israel stance. As I noted in Chapter 3, it was President Trump, more than any president in recent history, who showed kindness and support for the nation of Israel. This took the form of both personal and political actions. For example, in the former case, Trump was the first sitting president ever to visit the Western Wall.[116] Also, his own son-in-law, Jared Kushner, is a practicing Jew, thereby making Trump's own grandchildren at least part Jewish. From the political angle, Trump brokered four peace agreements between Arabs and Israel, he moved the US embassy to Jerusalem and recognized it as the capital of Israel, and Trump offered his support for Israel at the United Nations. This is important because no other nation has received more condemnations from the UN than Israel. As an example, according to *The Times of Israel*, in 2020 the UN condemned Israel 17 times compared to only six sanctions meted out for the rest of the world's countries combined![117] In June of 2018, Trump announced that the US "would leave the UN Human

Rights Council because of its anti-Israel bias. This made America the first country ever to leave the Council."[118] The hostility towards Israel at the UN is palpable and should not be overlooked for what it is. It is antisemitism and it is only getting worse. Using Israel as a scapegoat for all the Middle East's (and the world's) problems is not only dangerous, but it will also lead to a second Holocaust if we are not careful. Once Trump was removed from office, the Biden-Harris regime resumed the standoffish behavior against Israel first enacted by Obama. Not surprisingly, since Biden took over, all hell has broken loose in Israel and in America when it comes to the rise of antisemitism.

American Support for a "Third Intifada"

In the late spring of 2021, the Iranian-backed Palestinian terror organization known as Hamas began launching thousands of rockets from the Gaza Strip into Israel, many in the direction of Jerusalem. While the struggle between the Jewish and the Arab peoples is nothing new, what is new is how those in the West, particularly America and Canada, reacted to this event. I watched dumbfounded as American and Canadian city streets erupted in protest, not against Hamas, but rather against Israel! Antisemitism was no longer hidden in the dark areas of our society it was front and center with the news reels covering the protests in a celebratory manner. Then the antisemitism took on an even darker tone. Roving mobs supporting Hamas began searching for Jewish people and beating them in the streets. Once again, recall my analogy of the whirlwind rotating around a central axis. The cadre of antisemitic activists were drawing all the useful idiots and hate groups towards their cause. For those of us watching alternative conservative media, many of these stories were covered in a way that presented the protests for what they truly were: antisemitic. Meanwhile, I was amazed, but not surprised, at the almost complete silence of the MSM. The blatant displays of antisemitism on America's streets did not fit their narrative, which is that *Israel* is the problem with the Middle East, not the hostile Palestinians and Arabs. The actor Jon Voight posted a poignant message in the midst of the chaos. He minced no words addressing the leftist liberals who were attacking Jews in America; he called them fools and a "disgrace to this planet earth" for their actions and for not understanding their history. He forcefully reminded them of what happened to the Jews during WWII and how God views and protects His people. He concluded by saying to the liberal leftists, "you antisemitic fools will pay the price when God intervenes."[119] I could not agree with Mr. Voight more.

The same antisemitism is rearing its ugly head in Congress surrounding the ongoing Palestinian-Israeli conflict. When the Republican members of Congress sought to send aid for Israel's Iron Dome defense system, which they needed to shoot down incoming Hamas rockets, the Democrats voted in lockstep to block it.[120] This is the same thing they did earlier when the Republicans tried to pass a bill placing sanctions on Hamas and to stop any funding to the terrorist group. Again, the Democrats voted as a block to stop the legislation.[121] As the conflict dragged on, Biden was paralyzed to do anything. What side would he take? If he sided with the Jewish people many in his party would be enraged because of their support for the Palestinians. Instead of making any decisive statement, the Biden-Harris administration sat idly by until the conflict was nearing its end, or at least a ceasefire had been reached. It was then he stepped in and claimed he played a vital role in bringing an end to the hostilities, a blatant falsehood. I reiterate again that there is no place for antisemitism in any culture, especially in America and Canada, two countries that are home to so many immigrants who have fled countries because of oppression.

The reason for the rise of antisemitism in the West in fourfold. First, as noted in my previous chapter, when a culture rejects God is it any surprise that they would reject the nation who is "God's chosen people"? The natural outworking of this rejection of God is that Americans no longer read the Bible. This in turn leads to people not knowing how Israel became a nation devoted to their God. Even if the modern nation of Israel is more of a reflection of a secular democracy than it is the chosen people of God of the Bible, that does not diminish God's love and care for His people and His commitment to His covenant with them, despite their rejection of Him. For those of us who read the Bible closely, this cannot be missed, nor can it be sidestepped by the Church because of the damnable heresy of replacement theology. I will return to this in a moment. For now, it is important to realize that the Enemy hates God's people and the Enemy dwells in the hearts of those who have rejected God (John 8:44). We have sown the wind in this regard and now we are reaping the whirlwind. When we reject God for the alternative of imbibing rationalism and postmodern drivel, we turn into a society that reflects what it has become: Godless. A natural outworking of that is a rejection of what God finds most precious: His people.

A second concern is that the Church, especially the mainstream church in America, has adopted what is known as "replacement theology" (or Supersessionism) as a means of explaining Israel's relationship to the Church. Put simply, those proposing this heresy believe that the New Covenant established by Jesus has replaced the Old Covenant with Israel. Therefore, the Church takes the place of geo-political Israel and now the Church is all that matters to God. What is more, all the promises of God to Israel in the OT now belong to the Church. Sure, they will argue that Jewish people are important, but no more so than any other non-believers who need God. I can recall during my first master's program being invited out for supper with one of evangelicalism's leading OT ethicists. As we drove to our destination, I asked him the question about what role he thought geo-political Israel played in our current culture and for the end times. His response stunned me when he said modern Israel as a country is basically meaningless to God's greater plan for the world and for the Church. My immediate response, as a lowly student, was to allow my mind to run through the many OT passages speaking about the return of the Jewish people to their land, God's part in that process, and God's plan to bring the Jewish people as a group, remnant or otherwise, to a recognition of Jesus as Messiah (Zech 12:9–14). I also pondered the teachings of Paul in Romans 9–11 and his clear distinction between the time of the Gentiles and the future role of Israel. That conversation has stayed with me as I went on to complete two master's degrees and a PhD in the Hebrew Bible with a focus on the prophetic utterances of Ezekiel. To this day I am convinced that this scholar, and many of his ilk, was, and are, wrong. Unfortunately, the heretical theory has inundated the Church in America and is part of the evangelical vibe. When applied to modern political issues, proponents of this troubling theology take the side of the "underdog" or "oppressed" as of course Jesus, they argue, would do. They also support the "downtrodden" Palestinian people because they include a large population of Christian Palestinians. I have no problem praying for both groups, but when antisemitism grips even so-called Palestinian "Christians" then I question the nature of their salvation. Is it nominal only? When the Church marginalizes God's people in favor of a hostile segment of Muslim Arabs and Palestinians because of political and cultural expedience, we are quickly coming to a place of judgment. I would ask my fellow Christian supporters of the Palestinians, who continually launch unprovoked attacks on Israel: If the power differential was shifted and the Palestinians were in power, how do you think they would respond to Israel? You know exactly what the response would be. It would be the same as Hitler's! The Jewish people would be wiped off the face of the map in a heartbeat. Or consider what would happen to the "Christian" Palestinians if Hamas took control of all of Israel. They would be persecuted and killed in the same way ISIS destroyed some of the oldest Christian communities in Iraq and Syria. Israel is a shield for the Palestinian Christians against Islamic aggression. I am also concerned when the Church sides with the rest of culture in denouncing the Jews. When you are on the same side as radical Muslims and avowed anti-Semites, you may want to reconsider your stance.

The third reason for the rising antisemitism is our educational system, which has adopted Marxist ideology. As noted in Chapter 5, the progressives and Marxists have taken over almost all levels of our education system and have taught our youth for forty years to hate America, hate the Judeo-Christian God, and by extension, to hate His people, the Jews. It is important to keep in mind that a common trend in communist countries is to scapegoat the Jews. The natural progression is to start with antisemitism, move to marginalization of the group, and then ultimately to bring about the destruction of Jews by imprisonment and execution. As America adopts Marxism and communism, what do we expect will be the outcome? Another troubling trend in this regard is that there are numerous Christians who have adopted the troubling argument that they are not "communist" but merely "socialistic" in their political leanings. As I noted in an earlier chapter, socialism is not benign, it shares much in common with communist Marxism. The only difference is the fact that socialism is voting for government control of our lives whereas communism and Marxism generally take over by force. As we witnessed in the last American election, Marxist revolutionaries are now using a different type of coercion to get their way: they disguise their coercive activity under seemingly benign election "integrity" movements, but their goal is nothing less than outright voter fraud for the purpose of gaining control of America.

Finally, immigration has also played a key role in the rise of antisemitism. I have no problem with people coming from other countries to the United States as long as they assimilate. As noted in my previous chapter, without assimilation, racial tensions are easily stoked by radicals in our midst, especially those of the Muslim religion and political ideology.[122] I witnessed this firsthand in the country of my birth, Canada. Many people from eastern countries moved to Canada in the 1980s and 1990s and brought with them their centuries-old hostilities which in turned erupted in the cities where they settled. First- and second-generation Muslim immigrants to the US who hate Israel are finding a comfortable "home" among the leftists in the Democrat party. To be sure, the Democrats are now becoming the party of antisemitism with the likes of Ilhan Omar, Rashida Tlaib, Alexandria Ocasio-Cortez, and the political activist, and Palestinian Muslim, Linda Sarsour.[123] Whenever these, and others like them, speak about Israel it is evident that antisemitism undergirds their worldview. A clear example of this was when Rashida Tlaib stated in a May 11, 2019, interview that she gets a "calming feeling" when she thinks about the Holocaust.[124] Even though she insisted her words were taken out of context, Republicans were quick to denounce her comments as antisemitic. Similarly, Ilhan Omar minces no words about her antisemitism, and yet many Jewish people on the Left voted her into power. Omar regularly tweets her anti-semitism by saying things like "Israel has hypnotized the world," and it's about "the Benjamins baby," which was a reference to the hundred-dollar bill and her belief that the Jews are buying political power.[125] The hypocrisy of Omar's words was made public when undercover reporters with Project Veritas revealed that Omar is part of an illegal pay-to-vote scheme in part financed by Palestinians in an effort to have Omar support defunding Israel.[126] Not only is the scheme evidence of Omar's flouting of American election laws—making Minneapolis akin to the lawlessness of her country of birth, Somalia—but it shows her blatant antisemitic bias. I could go on with numerous examples but it is clear that Omar, Tlaib, and Sarsour are not isolated antisemitic activists and politicians. They are merely the most vocal. They are the "whirlwind" vortex and central axis around which other anti-Semites are coalescing. This is not just me being a fearmonger, Jewish Democrats themselves are also sounding the alarm.[127] Antisemitism is not just on the fringes of the Democrat party.[128] The rise of antisemitism can now be found at all levels of the Democrat Left and it is nowhere more evident than in the actions of BLM.

BLM's Antisemitism

As just noted, Marxist ideology leans naturally toward antisemitism. And as also noted, BLM is rooted in Marxist ideology that rejects the Judeo-Christian God, God's Word, and by extension, God's people. It came as no surprise that during the violent Palestinian uprising of 2021 by Hamas (see above), that the *New York Post* reported that BLM joined in solidarity with the terrorist group.[129] So-called fact checkers at *USA Today* retorted that BLM merely showed their support for the Palestinians.[130] I find it laughable that our liberal news outlets cannot grasp the reality that Hamas is in political power because they *are* Palestinians and elected by Palestinians, as if you can separate the two. Even though Hamas controls the Gaza Strip, and the Palestinian Authority controls the West Bank, they have an equal hate for Israel. Hamas is merely more vocal and violent in their attacks. Whatever group is fanning the flames of antisemitism, I would offer them a biblical example as a warning as to what their outcome will be.

A Biblical Warning to America

The book of Esther is an account relating a story of what happens to those who seek hostilities toward God's people. The story is centered around four main characters, Esther, Mordecai, Haman, and the Persian king, Ahasuerus. Because of Haman's enmity towards Mordecai, he devised a plot to have all the Jews in the Persian kingdom executed on a specific day. Haman was a direct descendant of Agag, an Amalekite king whom Samuel the prophet killed when Saul failed to do so as noted in 1 Samuel 15. Mordecai, on the other hand, was a direct descendant of Saul. The feud between the two people groups (Amalek and Israel) plays out in the story and boils over when Mordecai refuses to bow to Haman. In response, Haman encourages Ahasuerus to allow him to make a decree in the king's name and with his seal that all the Jews be killed on an appointed day because, Haman insists, this people group are troublesome and instigators of political uprisings. By the end of the story, Haman is hanged on the gallows he had erected to hang Mordecai. At the end of the account, Ahasuerus allows Mordecai and Esther to pass another decree, which states that the Jews can defend themselves against their enemies. On the day they are attacked, the Jews kill 75,000 of their enemies (Esther 9:16). While scholars have debated the historicity of the account, what is important to note is that the story clearly teaches that antisemitism will not be tolerated by God. This serves as a strong warning to America and those on the Left. God will judge those who are responsible for their hatred of God's people. If America does not take a stand and denounce the rising antisemitism in

America, we are doomed to repeat the same mistakes made by Haman, and Hitler.

Conclusion

Antisemitism is no laughing matter. Some may be reading this and thinking that I am sensationalizing a small fraction of the population. I would remind my readers to recall how thousands of anti-Semites gathered in Washington DC in May of 2021 to protest Israel's supposed oppression of the Palestinians.[131] Ironically, it is the Palestinians who are launching rockets into Israel and targeting civilians. Like the actions of the UN, many Arab Americans, along with both the uninformed "useful idiots" of the Left and those who have a clear agenda to marginalize Israel and seek their destruction, are coming together with a common goal: to bring about the demise of Israel. Such hatred will not go unchecked. God may allow antisemitism to fester and rear its ugly head for a time, but sooner or later He will have the final say. When we sow the wind of antisemitism, we will reap the whirlwind of God's judgment. Allowing antisemitism to swirl around the central vortex of the radical Left will bring about mass cultural devastation and possible destruction to the Jewish people. America is on a dangerous path and unless we repent, judgment is sure to follow. Again, those voting for a party that propagates antisemitism are complicit in the downward spiral of America. In many ways I feel like we are living what John the Revelator spoke about in Revelation. Are we now moving in that direction and seeing the fulfillment of the Revelator's prophetic words about the end times?

11

The Forecasted Thunderstorm: Are We Living the Book of Revelation?

As I noted in the introduction to Chapter 7, cloudbursts are something that can catch a person unprepared or off guard. Thunderstorms, on the other hand, are often forecasted days in advance by meteorologists who foresee the colliding of two pressure systems. Because of the foreseeable nature of thunderstorms, most can be prepared for. Like the warnings offered by meteorologists concerning a coming thunderstorm, throughout this book we have attempted to offer a warning of what is sure to take place unless America repents of its sin. We have based much of what we have presented upon the Word of God and His immutable nature of holiness and God's need to judge sin. God has also given us clear warnings of coming disasters which will accompany the end times. Prophetic texts and biblical parallels and examples offer the reader a picture of what is to come in the end times. The book of Revelation is one such book despite the notoriously challenging interpretive

issues surrounding much of the text. Even with the interpretive diffi-
culties, most scholars agree that the book presents a picture of aspects
of the coming eschaton. Others agree that the picture of God's judgment is not just a portrait for the first-century audience but is also
reflective of things to come.

I grew up in the era of Hal Lindsey's *The Late Great Planet Earth*
(1970), David Wilkerson's prophetic pronouncements found in *Set the
Trumpet to Thy Mouth* (1993), and the music of Larry Norman, "I Wish
We'd All Been Ready" (1969). Authors, evangelists, and musicians of
that era spoke of the end times and Jesus' "soon" return. I remember
the feeling of anticipation and the uneasiness that accompanied the
reading, viewing, or hearing of these types of messages. I can recall
wondering if I would live to see my twenties before Jesus returned.
Would I ever finish school? Would I ever have the chance to get married
before it all ended? These and many similar questions swirled around
in my head as I grew up in the turbulent period of the 70s, 80s, and
90s. Looking back today on those times in light of the cultural changes
in the West we are facing now I can confidently say that we are closer
today than ever before to Jesus' Second Coming. We are faced with a
culture of corruption and perversion like never before. We are living
in a period when people regularly defame the name of God and mock
many of our foundational Judeo-Christian beliefs as being passé. As I
have noted in previous publications, we are tearing down ethical and
moral fences at a record pace. This cannot continue with impunity. Our
corrupt and godless politicians are passing laws that undermine the
holiness of God and His clearly defined boundaries in His holy Word.
Americans of every stripe are flaunting their sinfulness without shame.
Most churches no longer teach on sin and the coming judgment. In
light of these and many other anti-God and anti-biblical actions can
we say that we are witnessing the book of Revelation? Put differently,
are we now *living* the book of Revelation?

In this chapter I will attempt to answer this question based upon
recent developments in America and the wider global scene. However,
I will answer this question by offering my reader a series of other

questions to ponder. While any one event or concern may not be tantamount to confirming God's judgment on America, when viewed as a whole, I am more convinced than ever that God's judgment is not just impending, it is upon us already. Indeed, several warnings from the book of Revelation appear to be unfolding before our eyes.

Are There Similarities Between the Biblical Warnings and Today's America?

The author of Revelation primarily used two prophetic books from the OT, Daniel and Ezekiel, to describe the coming eschatological judgment upon the earth. To be sure, Ezekiel and Daniel's imagery and prophetic utterances underpin the arc of the book of Revelation. One of these utterances deals with the Antichrist. In this vein, Ezekiel speaks of a coming ruler by the name of Gog, the prince of Rosh, Meshech, and Tubal, who will attack God's people (Ezek 38:3; cf. Rev 20:8). Similarly, in his vision of the empires of the world in Daniel 7, which is parallel to Nebuchadnezzar's dream of the giant statue in chapter 2, Daniel also speaks about a coming world ruler. He says, "And he shall speak *great* words against the most High, and shall wear out the saints of the most High, and think to change times and laws: and they shall be given into his hand until a time and times and the dividing of time" (Dan 7:25; KJV). John likewise discusses this man of sin in Revelation 13. Many have identified this coming ruler as the Antichrist (2 Thess 2:3–4; 1 John 2:18). Not surprisingly, many of the situations surrounding the coming of the Antichrist seem to be unfolding in America today. While the Lawless one has not been revealed yet, the spirit of anti-christ is certainly present in America. For example, we have a culture and political elites who blaspheme God daily. Also, we have governing elites and cultural movements that desire to "change times and laws" to fit their agenda which is anti-God. The Judeo-Christian principles and patriotism of America is on life support and taking its last breaths unless God extends mercy.

Did the Revelator Foresee Our Modern Predicament?

There are numerous connections we could make between the events recorded in the book of Revelation and what we are experiencing around the globe today. I am not attempting to predict the end times with the Bible in one hand and a newspaper in the other. This was a common methodological approach of the end times prophets from my childhood as I noted above. Nevertheless, Jesus did say we would know the season when the Son of Man would return (Matt 24:32–33). As such, we can look at the Scriptures and see direct parallels between what the Revelator saw through the Spirit's impartation and what we are experiencing today. I will offer a few points of contact before delving into a more detailed discussion of broader synchronisms in the next few sections.

First, John opens his book by noting the numerous issues with the seven churches of Asia Minor. Two of the key issues were depravity and lukewarmness in the churches at Thyatira (Rev 2:18–21) and Laodicea (Rev 3:14–18) respectively. As I have noted throughout and elsewhere, the modern Church is on dangerous footing because of the acceptance of sexual ethics contrary to the Word of God and because of our luke-warmness to the things of God and to His Word. As church attendance declines, and Christians become more enculturated away from biblical values, the picture of John's opening chapters in Revelation mirrors what is going on in America today.

Second, John noted that in the end times an army numbering 200 million would arise from the east and be a part of the destruction of one third of the population of the world (Rev 9:15–16). I cannot help but make the connections to the militancy of China and the vast numbers of their armies which are virulently atheistic and anti-Israel. We are living in a period of history when the elites in Washington are siding with China in many areas of diplomacy and failing to recognize the dangers that they pose. China has global ambitions and as the US removes itself from the Middle East and foreign affairs there, China is filling the gap. I will return to the dangers posed by China in a separate section below.

Third, as I noted in Chapter 10, the rise of antisemitism in America and around the globe is evidence that the people of Israel will be left alone to defend themselves in the end times. The prophet Zechariah (see chapters 12–14) foresaw this and so did Daniel and John the Revelator. Both Daniel and John note that the Devil will seek to destroy the saints/people of God, that is, Israel (Dan 7:24–27; Rev 13:7). Revelation chapter 12 highlights the Devil's antisemitic and anti-God campaign that has been going on for some time but will increase during the end times. While God will protect His people from total annihilation, it is clear that we are quickly approaching a time when public opinion in the West, and America in particular, is turning against God's people. Indeed, we are doing the bidding of Lucifer himself when it comes to political and public attacks on Israel.

Finally, the increasing numbers of plague-like events throughout the world finds several parallels with what we read in Revelation concerning the bowl, vial, and trumpet judgments. For example, when Covid shut down the global economy more than one person noted the parallels and wondered if we were living in the end times. I think we definitely are. In fact, I believe the Covid pandemic was a test run for coming events whereby governments or world leaders will exert complete control of the populace. Some scientists are sounding a warning that the Covid-19 vaccine will change people's immune system to the point that it will not allow a person to fight off other infections and viruses.[132] This would mean that in the future, people will be susceptible to these new infections, which will cause global death or injury. One wonders if this is the word spoken by John in Revelation when God says one third of the world's population will die (Rev 9:18)! Others are saying it's an issue of control and tracking; it is the beginning of controlling people's behavior such as travel and commerce.[133] Recently I saw a comment on social media that read "With all these states now getting together and offering Vaxx recipients prizes, gifts, lottery winnings, and special privileges, it's starting to sound lots like satan saith unto him, 'All these things I will give thee, if thou wilt fall down and worship me' (Matt 4:9 KJV)."[134]

Are We Being Prepared for the Coming Antichrist?

In Chapter 8, my wife, Christine, examined the circumstances surrounding and stemming from the Covid-19 pandemic as an example of how America is quickly turning into a totalitarian state. The truth is, more than a decade ago, elites laid out how they could use a pandemic to control the masses. In 2010, a report was drafted by a thinktank and sponsored by the Rockefeller Foundation outlining a hypothetical scenario that described a global pandemic very similar to the Covid-19 pandemic.[135] In the report, the hypothetical pandemic would be used to strip people of their rights and to program people to give up rights willingly in the name of safety. Again, as Christine noted about the words of our founding father Benjamin Franklin, "Those who would give up essential Liberty, to purchase a little temporary Safety, deserve neither Liberty nor Safety."

This is important because according to the books of 1 and 2 Thessalonians, one of the lies of the period of the Antichrist is that his rule will bring peace and safety to the world. Paul says, "Now as to the times and the epochs, brethren, you have no need of anything to be written to you. For you yourselves know full well that the day of the Lord will come just like a thief in the night. While they are saying, 'Peace and safety!' then destruction will come upon them suddenly like birth pangs upon a woman with child; and they shall not escape" (1 Thess 5:1–3; NASB). We are willingly giving up our freedoms for the sake of "safety" and in doing so we are surrendering our liberties to the government which will one day take away more than we ever bargained for. Safety and security sound good but the truth is that in a fallen world there are no guarantees like this. We have to rely on God and trust in His protection as well. One of the other areas where we are quickly seeing a push for security is in our financial transactions. Because of our increased use of cashless purchasing, the Enemy will use this to his advantage to gain complete control of our ability to buy and sell. Once again, this sounds eerily similar to John's warnings in Revelation 13.

Is the Enemy Preparing Us for a Cashless Society?

"And there was given to him to give breath to the image of the beast, that the image of the beast might even speak and cause as many as do not worship the image of the beast to be killed. And he causes all, the small and the great, and the rich and the poor, and the free men and the slaves, to be given a mark on their right hand, or on their forehead, and *he provides* that no one should be able to buy or to sell, except the one who has the mark, *either* the name of the beast or the number of his name. Here is wisdom. Let him who has understanding calculate the number of the beast, for the number is that of a man; and his number is six hundred and sixty-six" (Rev 13:15–18; NASB).

Back in 2012 I taught a survey of the NT class at the freshman level. As I was preparing my class on the book of Revelation, I found an on-line video showing the coming ease with which people could be micro-chipped in order to eliminate the use of cash. At the time this seemed like a distant future concept. Now the use of cryptocurrencies is on the rise. Many see this as the way of the future where all transactions will be electronic. As of July 2021, eighty different central banks worldwide are moving in this direction.[136] The system is being set up for a one-world monetary system. How will this be instituted? It will be sold as a means of safety and security and as an important part of our ability to travel freely. Let me explain what I mean by these two points.

While writing this book, I woke up one morning and saw that one online user noted that Microsoft has patented a new chip that will be used to track data from one's body for use with cryptocurrency. The patent number is 666.[137] Sure, this may be a mere coincidence or is it the Enemy once again rubbing our noses in the reality of what is coming upon the earth? The die is cast and the powers that be will use this technology to house all our data. Social security numbers, banking and

medical information (vaccination records included) and any other pertinent personal data will be a part of the new system. This, of course, is
very close to what we read about in the book of Revelation chapter 13.[138]
You may be thinking that this is impossible, but the US Congress has
already introduced legislation proposed as a means of tracking people
in the name of health safety. One such piece of legislation is HR6666
(2019–2020 116th Congress), which is designed for contact tracing for
the Covid-19 pandemic.

Think about this for a moment. During the Covid crisis we were
encouraged not to use cash. This was to eliminate the possibility of
infecting others through contact with "contaminated" money. It made
sense but what are the natural outworkings of such thinking and policies? It is to prepare us for the argument that we need to move to a
cashless society for our own "safety."

This is the same type of argument now being made for the Covid
vaccine shots. Now Covid vaccine passports are being pushed by many
which will be needed to travel, do commerce, work, or even buy food!
Does this sound familiar? On top of this, in July of 2021, the Biden
administration announced that they were going to start going door-to-
door to push vaccination for Covid-19.[139] This is all part of making lists
of people who are and are not onboard with the government's plan.[140]
Recently on CNN's Chris Cuomo's show, a female guest pointed out
that the opening of states must be tied to vaccination. She noted that if
the government did not catch this opportunity to allow people to have
"freedoms" after vaccination, people will take it anyway. We are being
programmed to accept government issued IDs and certificates to do our
basic living. The mark of the beast does not sound so crazy anymore.

This is not just for areas of government oversight. Now churches are
throwing people out of their buildings for not wearing a mask. As I
noted in Chapter 4, in one case in Texas, a pregnant and nursing mom
was thrown out of church with a threat of arrest for not wearing a
mask. The irony is that the main pastor called the police (three officers
responded) on the parishioner and the usher egged on the police as she
was being removed. The woman ended up being permanently banned

from the church, convicted of "trespassing."[141] People now put more trust in "the science" than they do in God. They are being driven by an unhealthy fear. Will these types of plagues and hyped circumstances be the thing that causes "men's hearts to fail them for fear"? (Luke 21:26). This verse from Luke comes from Jesus' teaching on his Second Coming and in fact is the verse before the last statement noting this very event.

Will People Actually Worship Satan?

In Revelation 13:15 John states, "And there was given to him to give breath to the image of the beast, that the image of the beast might even speak and cause as many as do not worship the image of the beast to be killed" (Rev 13:15; NASB). Many may be thinking they would never worship Satan or any of his cohorts. The truth is throughout history God-fearing people have been threatened with death and even killed for their refusal to bow to idol images or to worship false gods. I would point my reader to Daniel chapter 3 as a fine example. Today, America thinks the existence of Satan is the punchline of a joke. They toy with the idea that God can be mocked, and Satan can be controlled. This is part of the Enemy's campaign to make God "uncool" or appear non-existent. Young people are being programmed to think hanging out with Satan and being a part of his "team" is the place to be. I offer two examples with a similar theme.

First, in 2021, rapper Lil Nas X in conjunction with the company MSCHF released a limited edition of Nike sneakers dedicated to Satan. The sneaker came with a pentagram medallion and mockingly included the biblical reference Luke 10:18: "I saw Satan fall from heaven as a lightning bolt." The campaign slogan had the tag line it is "better to reign in hell than to serve in heaven," which comes from Milton's *Paradise Lost*.[142] Each of the 666 pairs of sneakers included a drop of human blood. The promotion was part of the rapper's campaign for his new album. In one of the videos, the rapper is depicted giving a lap dance to Satan and then killing him. The message is clear, Satan is a joke and easily conquered. This is the position of fools. While Nike sued the company that altered and sold the shoes, the depravity of our entertainment industry and populace is telling. The limited supply of sneakers priced at over $1000.00 each sold out in minutes online.

The second example is connected to the same rapper. During the Easter season, the comedy show, Saturday Night Live, did a "comedy" routine depicting an actor portraying the same rapper giving a lap dance not to Satan, but to an actor playing the role of God. At the end of the profane skit, one of the other "comedians" shouts, "Happy Easter everyone!"[143] This is the blasphemy that is being pawned off on Americans as "entertainment." Christians need to take a stand and say enough is enough. However, because Christians actually watch this garbage, I believe it is just another sign of the weakness of our Christian walk and the reason why judgment is coming to our nation. It no longer would be a surprise to me that many in America would willingly serve Satan and take his mark in order to survive in a "book-of-Revelation world."

Are We in the Last Days?

Back in Jesus' day, the disciples asked Jesus a poignant question about his return: "When will these things [that is, the events of the end times] be?" In fact, all three of the Synoptic Gospels record this very question (Matt 24:3; Mark 13:4; Luke 21:7). I certainly am not going to lay out a specific date for Jesus' return. Jesus warns about doing this very thing in the same chapter in which he spoke about his Second Coming (Matt 24:36). Yet, that does not stop us from speculating on the *season* of Jesus' return. Jesus warned his disciples in Matthew 24 to be prepared by knowing the signs of the times. In light of this encouragement from Jesus, I would like to put forward three different pieces of evidence that seem to point to the reality that we are closer to the coming of Jesus than many may think. To be sure, Jesus also said that his Second Coming would catch most people off guard (Matt 24:50). The three pieces of evidence come from three different venues: one is sociological, one is geo-political, and one is Scriptural.

The sociological example comes from the work of Joseph Daniel

Unwin which he compiled in the 1930s. In his book *Sex and Culture* (1934), Unwin examined the collapse of 86 cultures and empires over a 5000-year period of history.[144] In his research he found that every cultural collapse had a similar trajectory and pattern, which could be detected based upon their last three generations of existence. For reference, Unwin's generation equaled 33 years. The pattern included the common trait that in the first of these last three generations, each culture moved away from sexual chastity and constancy especially among the females in the population. This loosening of sexual ethics was marked by allowing premarital sex and openness within marriage (polygamy, open marriages, etc.). In this first generation, the newfound sexual freedom was exhilarating and liberating, or so it seemed. The culture seemed unhindered by the change and appeared to be flourishing. However, by the second generation the culture or empire began to witness the negative effects of their loosened sexual ethics as the culture began to reject not just their sexual morality, but their religious and cultural history including their worship and devotion to their deities. Put differently, cracks began to form in their traditional culture both spiritually and secularly. By the time the culture moved into the third and final generation, the culture had devolved to a lowest common denominator where people thought only of their own self-interests and needs as opposed to those of the larger culture; they rejected their religious past; they moved away from rationalistic thinking; and their sexual ethic was pretty much non-existent. It was in this third generation that *every* culture collapsed or was conquered by another culture with a higher sexual ethic. Unwin also noticed that cultures with a high sexual ethic that prohibited sex before and outside of marriage flourished and expanded both culturally and geographically. They excelled in science and in the arts. Conversely, those in the third generation of decline regressed in these areas.

When Unwin's model is applied to America the pattern becomes shockingly prophetic. Our sexual revolution began in the 1960s whereby our sexual ethics began to loosen among both men and women. Indeed, the women's liberation movement marked this newfound shift in our culture with women flouting their newfound sexual freedom. According to Unwin's generational pattern, 1960–1993 would account for this first generation of "freedom."[145] Not surprisingly, this is the same period when all the sexual proclivities of America burst forth upon the nation and people reveled in their newfound freedom from former sexual taboos. Everything appeared to be on an upward trajectory of freedom and liberty in this regard. Yet, according to Unwin, this is a false sense of security and freedom. The second generation is when each culture began to experience the cracks in their foundation. They rejected their religious and historical heritage and began to devolve as a culture. Again, this is "prophetic" when we look at what has happened in our "second" generation from 1994–2027. As America comes to the end of its second-generation timespan, everything noted by Unwin in his research of past cultures and empires is coming to pass. We are devolving as a culture as we are headed for civil war (at least a cold civil war). We are witnessing the rejection and destruction of our history, both religious and secular. Think about the tearing down of statues, the rejection of America as a great nation, the rewriting of history with the so-called 1619 project, the rise of CRT to turn races against each other, the proliferation of degrading and abominable sex-education programs to younger and younger children, and a complete rejection of the Judeo-Christian principles of our nation's founding not to mention the rejection of our God. The perfect storm is upon us. According to Unwin's pattern, the final generation for America will be from 2028–2061. I would argue that the predicted period of collapse is already upon us. We are quickly devolving into a self-interested, God-rejecting, lowest-common-denominator people as every person does what is right in their own eyes and seeks only their own good. And even on the state level, we have an increasing number of states that want to secede from the Union because of our deep moral and ethical divisions. Indeed, numerous states are already restricting governmental travel to other states because of their "oppressive" sexual ethics. California alone has restricted travel to close to twenty other states because these (mostly "Red" states) embrace traditional values! Civil War may not be here yet, but deep divides continue to grow in America most of which are rooted in the devolving of our sexual ethics and values. Put simply, Red states are now at odds with Blue states. What is left? According to Unwin, we will collapse as a culture, or we will be conquered by another culture with a higher sexual morality. Is it possible we are witnessing that even now as China and Islam seek to take over America? This brings me to my next piece of evidence, the geo-political vector.

It is no secret that China and Islam want to see the demise of America or at least its overthrow. As I noted in an earlier chapter, Islam plays the long game and the chances of them being solely responsible for America's overthrow in the next 30–40 years is perhaps slim. This does not mean, however, that they will not join with another world power like China to bring about the downfall of America. During the Trump administration this was virtually impossible because Trump sought to turn America around and return it to its past glory with a focus on its proud history and Judeo-Christian values and heritage. Trump sought to marginalize China and take them to task for their unfair trade practices. After the 2020 election, China boasted of having regained control of America through their China-friendly proxies in the US government and among the financial elite (that is, Biden and Wall Street).[146]

What is becoming increasingly clear is that China has every intention of controlling not just America, but the world. In fact, they have made the pledge to do it by 2049, the centennial of the Chinese Communist revolution when Mao Zedong took power. China has had their plan—what is called the "Hundred-Year Marathon"—in place for half a century now.[147] Once they gain control economically, they will force compliance upon other nations through military dominance,[148] a position that is quickly coming to fruition. China has stolen intellectual and trade secrets and the West has aided in their rise by investing in their economy with the false hope that they will become capitalistic and join the rest of the nations of the world as a respectable contributor. But this is all a ruse. China is developing super weapons that can counter America's military weapons systems. Known as the "Assassin's Mace," China is now developing smart weapons which are much cheaper than conventional weapons. These weapons include electromagnetic pulse (EMP) devices, microwave, laser, anti-satellite, and particle beam technologies.[149]

From a political perspective, what is happening now since the 2020 election is nothing less than frightening as there is clear evidence, whether the MSM wants to admit it or not, that China was involved in manipulating the 2020 election to get Biden into office. Biden is a puppet of China based upon Biden and his son's illegal interactions and business dealings that have compromised the presidency of the US. With America's withdrawal from Afghanistan, now China has a straight geographical path to march to the Middle East. Not surprisingly, China and the Taliban are becoming close allies in the region. People may think I am fearmongering, but if we do not secure our elections and push back against the aggression of China, then America is certainly doomed to its fate. I also find it telling that China is now aiding Islamic nations in the Middle East since America has withdrawn and left a power vacuum. Do not get me wrong, China and Islam have nothing in common, just look at the Uyghur situation. But like the radical Left in America and its unholy alliance with Islam, they have a common enemy: the sovereignty of America based upon its strong Judeo-Christian founding as a sovereign country. Again, note the date of China's goal to dominate the world; it is 2049. This date falls within the closing portion of my predicted third generation according to Unwin's pattern which I noted above. While this may be overwhelming and fanciful to some, let me offer one final line of argumentation and one final piece of evidence: the Scriptural one.

As I noted in the opening of this chapter, I grew up being told that the end of the world would come by 1988 based upon Jesus' words in Matthew 24:32–34. Jesus says, "Now learn the parable from the fig tree: when its branch has already become tender, and puts forth its leaves, you know that summer is near; even so you too, when you see all these things, recognize that He is near, *right* at the door. Truly I say to you, this generation will not pass away until all these things take place" (NASB; compare Mark 13:28; Luke 21:29). Many prophetic voices of the past made the link between the fig tree and Israel as a nation and put this connection forward as evidence that the return of Israel to her land in 1948 marked the countdown of the final generation. Scholars insisted that the biblical generation was a 40-year timespan. The problem with this prediction was that nowhere do we find Scriptural evidence confirming the 40-years-equals-one-generation argument. Now, do not get me wrong, I think the fig tree parable may very well be a reference to Israel based upon other passages that seem to intimate the connection (Jer 8:13; Hosea 9:10; Joel 1:7; 2:22; Matt 21:19; Mark 11:13–21; Luke 13:6–9). However, the 40-year connection is problematic as we saw at the end of the twentieth century when nothing happened eschatologically.

When we step back away from the text of Matthew 24, Mark 13, and Luke 21, is there any place that can offer us insight into what Jesus was referencing when he spoke of "this generation not passing away until all these things were fulfilled"? I believe the answer is in the opening book of the Bible: Genesis. There is only one place to my knowledge where God Himself identifies the length of a generation and that is in Genesis 15:16. Here God equates the 400 years of 15:13 to four generations of Abraham's descendants. In this case, a generation is equal to 100 years. What is also of interest is that God's prophetic word is speaking about Israel coming out of a time of exile in Egypt and entering into the promised land of Canaan as a possession. When Israel returned to their land in 1948, this marked their return from exile among the nations (see Ezekiel 34–37) to their promised home. If we apply this 100-year span to Israel's return in 1948, which would be 2048, we once again find a striking parallel with Unwin's prediction and China's declaration of world dominance. If I am correct in my calculations, then we are quickly approaching the final days of America and of world history. My declaration of this rapidly approaching coming of God's judgment fits with what I have been saying throughout and with what many prophets are saying about Jesus' soon return.

Conclusion

The book of Revelation is certainly a troubling book for most who read it. Its apocalyptic genre and end time scenarios are hard to read. Death, destruction, Satan, the rise of the Antichrist and the False Prophet all lend to the dismal predictions of the world's final days. However, I did not write this chapter to scare people but rather to get them thinking about what is laying ahead in the immediate future. The collapse of our sexual ethics, our rejection of God, the changes in American (and world!) politics, and many national governments' coercion of people to follow the "science" and accept Big Brother and Big Government's strategies for a "successful life" do not give me much hope, they smack of the end times as outlined in the book of Revelation. And if the three pieces of argumentation I noted immediately above are accurate, then we are about to enter the final generation which will be marked by the collapse of America, and no doubt the freedom of the world's peoples. Despite the gloom and the doom, however, many are prophesying that God is going to pour out His Spirit one last time and that God will bring in a final harvest by means of an end time's revival. To this, I posit a final question: are these prophets correct?

12

The Calm in the Eye of the Storm: Will There Be an End-Times Revival?

A hurricane is a storm with violent winds rotating around a central axis. Without fail, hurricanes destroy everything in their path when they reach landfall. The central axis of these types of severe weather phenomenon is called the "eye" of the storm. In the eye of a hurricane there is an eerie calm as the storm rages around on all sides off in the distance. Despite the period of calm in the eye of the storm, sooner or later the storm will continue moving and engulf that previously calm area unless the storm lifts or dissipates. While someone is in the eye of a storm, they may have enough time to get to a place of safety before the outer bands of the storm hit their place of dwelling and wreak havoc. Today we are witnessing the chaos of a gathering storm and in many ways, we are already seeing the effects of the cultural, political, and religious "storm" bearing down on America. In the midst of this chaos many are declaring that God is going to send an end-times revival to bring in a vast harvest before Jesus' return and before the time of "Jacob's trouble" unleashed by the Antichrist (Jer 30:7; Dan 12:1). It is believed that this revival or ingathering will allow people enough time to find spiritual "safety" from the storm that is bearing down on America. Are the prophets and those declaring such a revival, correct? In this chapter I will examine the possibility of these claims along with the biblical evidence to see if we should in fact expect an end-times revival. Put differently, will America experience a Fifth Great Awakening on par with the first four Great Awakenings of our past?

An Overview of the Great Awakenings

As I touched on in Chapter 9, the First Great Awakening took place in the 1730s and 1740s. This revival was marked by the stern and sterile preaching of clergymen like Jonathan Edwards (1703–1758) and George Whitefield (1714–1770). The Second Great Awakening took place between the 1790s and the 1840s and was sparked by the ministry of John (1703–1791) and Charles Westley (1707–1788) and was followed by the ministry of Charles Finney (1792–1875). According to some, there was a Third Great Awakening that took place from the late 1860s to the early twentieth century (ca. 1920s). There were two parts to this awakening, one more "liberal" in its focus and one more "conservative." The former movement was more focused on a postmillennial eschatology rooted in the social gospel movement of mainline churches. Many in this camp at this time believed that the Church could make the world so civilized and God-fearing that this utopia would usher in Christ's return at which time Jesus would establish his millennial kingdom on earth. Of course, the level of wholesale slaughter witnessed during the First World War among the supposed "enlightened" societies of Europe dashed any hopes of a rational world-wide utopia, which would usher in Jesus' second return. The second prong of the Third Great Awakening was more conservative in its bent and was marked by the ministry and teaching of D.L. Moody (1837–1899) and later by the fiery preaching of Billy Sunday (1862–1935). During this time, the holiness movement emerged which in turn sparked the Pentecostal outpouring in the first two decades of the twentieth century. At that time, we also witnessed the birth of world evangelism through the missionary and the Bible-School movements. Finally, some have proposed that a Fourth Great Awakening took place in post-WWII America up to the 1970s with the work of revivalists and evangelists like Billy Graham (1918–2018). However one assesses the great awakenings of the past, namely, whether there were two, three, or four, we are now being told that a final revival or awakening of sorts will take place prior to Jesus' return enabling a final great harvest. Unfortunately, the only awakening I am seeing currently is a false awakening being fanned by the ungodly and atheistic Left.

The False Awakening of "Wokeness"

God made all of us spiritual beings in need of a Savior. The desire to find spiritual fulfillment is innate, but many seek it through false paths. In his recent book, *God's Chaos Code*, social commentator and spiritual leader, Lance Wallnau, noted that during a stump speech for the Biden-Harris ticket, Obama praised the "great awakening" taking place among the youth of America.[150] Wallnau is indeed correct when he notes that this "great awakening" of the Left is not good, it is evil in its origins. America is in the beginning stages of this counterfeit awakening, and it is gaining speed and sweeping the entire nation. This is coming in the form of cultural "wokeness" for the purpose of bringing "salvation" to the downtrodden through social justice movements (see more in Chapter 7 above). But the wokeness of our society is not one that will lead to spiritual salvation. It is a false revival and awakening that leads to death. This is leading to unrest and chaos in America, as opposed to the true peace that comes when Jesus changes one's life.[151] The Enemy knows this all too well and is therefore making every effort to convince secular America, and even some self-professing Christians, that he has an equally effective answer to their longing for spiritual fulfillment. Left unchecked, this counterfeit great awakening will not lead to spiritual freedom and awareness, it will lead to deepening divisions within our country and perhaps even to a civil war.

Will There Be a Final Revival?

Despite this apparent counterfeit awakening, many prophets and pastors are still declaring that there will be one final genuine awakening that will bring about an ingathering before the great and terrible day of the Lord. Like my wife and I have been doing in this book, many spiritually likeminded individuals are declaring the dire circumstances America is facing and the urgency of the hour. Wallnau puts it this way, "Heaven is revealing the root and the fruit of what we are up against as a nation and God is laying the axe to the root of the tree. Our nation is sick, and without an extension of God's mercy—and time—we face the premature death of America."[152] While Wallnau and others continue to be optimistic that God will indeed act soon, I am becoming more convinced each day that America's best days are behind her, and that the end is quickly approaching. Put simply, I am not convinced that the Church is in the position to respond to God's move of the Spirit, nor do I feel the Church is willing to do what it takes to foster a spiritual awakening anywhere near on par with those of the past. We have a Church that continues to compromise its position on holiness, on sexual ethics, on the authority of God's Word, and on the value of church attendance. The Church no longer reads God's Word, pastors do not preach it in its fullness let alone preach on sin. Our services are nothing more than pep rallies used to pump the saints up for an hour or more once a week only to have them walk out the doors and continue living the way they did before they entered the sanctuary on Sunday or Wednesday. Christians may not admit to it, but they simply do not want to take the time to foster their faith in God and their knowledge of the Word.

I speak as someone who has been attending, teaching at, or working in Christian institutions for more than 25 years. What I have witnessed is a rapid decline in fervency among believers and this despite the fact that we are living in the midst of some of the most Godless and God-rejecting cultural trends in my short lifetime. Back in the mid-to-late 90s the handwriting was already on the wall as I witnessed church after church close their doors on Sunday nights and opt for a "small group" setting for fellowship—or nothing at all—as opposed to the once-common revival service on Sunday evening. I remember as a child and young adult that the Sunday evening service was the time when people were encouraged to invite their unsaved loved ones and friends to church in order to hear a "salvation" message. I remember the altar services of tarrying for hours until we heard from God. I can remember looking out on the congregation on a Sunday night as the seats would be full of worshiping believers. I recall the rear doors of the church remaining wide open during the hot summer months as the sounds of singing praises to God filtered out onto the silent streets. Of course, this was the period leading up to the "prophesied" date of 1988 and the expected soon-return of Jesus at any moment (see my earlier discussion). Yet, even with this eschatological focus back then, there still was a sense of urgency which permeated the Church and a desire to see souls saved and changed for the glory of God.

For clarification, I am not longing for a nostalgic return to some mythological version of the past but rather a return to a fervent urgency of seeking God in light of the hour in which we live. My wife and I attend a large church of close to 800 people. We also attend one of the available small groups on Sunday nights. I often teach on Wednesday evenings when our church offers educational classes for the congregation. I, along with several other former pastors as well as professors from the local Christian university, offer our expertise to our local church in order to teach the attendees about the Bible and/ or the coming storm of God's judgment. While I have witnessed a faithful remnant attending these classes, it is but a drop in the bucket compared to the hundreds of parishioners who show up on a Sunday morning. If we have a hundred or so people show up for the variety of classes being offered, this is considered a "good" night. Where are all the "faithful" believers who crowd the sanctuary on a Sunday morning to hear the latest singing group, visiting evangelist, pastor's sermon series, or the Christmas or Easter cantatas? Apparently, they have other more important things to do than make sure their children are in church or that they avail themselves of well-trained teachers. I do not like to say it, but they are either willing to revel in their biblical and spiritual ignorance, or they simply cannot be bothered. Either way, this is not the picture of a Church that is ready for a revival or that is even willing to be on the cutting edge of it.

Do not get me wrong, I think God can pour out His Spirit whenever He so chooses, and I pray that those proclaiming an end-time revival are correct in their assessment. But when I look at the biblical witness and what it teaches about the moving of God and His Spirit in moments similar to what we are experiencing in America, I see something very different. I see the salvation of a *remnant* as opposed to a great ingathering of masses of people. In the next section I will offer some of the biblical evidence that I see as informing my position that the end times may not be marked by a massive influx of unbelievers but rather a falling away of the saints.

Is There Biblical Evidence for an End-times Revival?

I have read the works of several authors proclaiming an end-times revival. One of the common approaches of these writers is their reliance on the Hebrew Scriptures for their biblical backing for their prophesied revival. I am torn as an OT professor at how these well-meaning prophets and pastors use the Hebrew Scriptures. I love the Hebrew Text and there is so much in it that is helpful for the child of God to be thoroughly furnished for every good work (2 Tim 3:16–17). This concern being noted, the book of Isaiah is a common go-to book because of its numerous passages relating to the final days of Israel. For example, we find in many places in Isaiah 54–57 a picture of a glorious return of God's people to their faith in Him. The problem with making a direct application of these texts to the Church is that these passages seem more suited to their actual context, namely, a message for the nation of *Israel* prior to the second return of Christ when the nation of Israel will return to their God (see also Zech 12–14). When I put these passages in their larger OT context, I find that God's judgment upon His people is never preceded by a revival, but rather by a falling away. The books of Judges and Kings are replete with examples. I know some may suggest that Josiah's reform from 640 609 BC is the exception to the rule, but this again must be read in light of its historical context. Even though Judah appeared to experience a revival of sorts prior to their exiles in 604, 597, and ultimately in 586 BC, when you read the book of Jeremiah, a prophet who lived through this very period, you find that the people were doing lip service to God as opposed to experiencing a genuine return to their God (see for example Jer 7:1–15). This is no less the case for the messages of other prophets of the period leading up to Judah's exile to Babylon (Joel 2:13; Micah 6:6–8).

Due to the focus of the OT prophets on the nation of Israel as opposed to the Church, I think it best to look at the NT to see what the authors writing in the period of the early church had to say about a coming end-time revival. I will begin with the words of Jesus in the gospel of Matthew. When Jesus gave his response to his disciples' request to know what Jesus' return would be like and what they were to expect, Jesus noted that the gospel would be preached to all nations (Matt 24:14). This does not signify a revival per se. What is important to our discussion is when Jesus went on to say that "As it was in the days of Noah, so shall also the coming of the Son of man be. For as in the days that were before the flood they were eating and drinking, marrying and giving in marriage, until the day that Noah entered into the ark, And the people knew not until the flood came, and took them all away; so shall also the coming of the Son of man be" (Matt 24:37–39; paraphrased from the KJV). This signifies a sudden return with most people unaware of the time of their visitation by God.

Paul also warned young Timothy of the way it will be in the last days. Paul says, "I charge *thee* therefore before God, and the Lord Jesus Christ, who shall judge the quick and the dead at his appearing and his kingdom; Preach the word; be instant in season, out of season; reprove, rebuke, exhort with all longsuffering and doctrine. For the time will come when they will not endure sound doctrine; but after their own lusts shall they heap to themselves teachers, having itching ears; And they shall turn away *their* ears from the truth, and shall be turned unto fables" (2 Tim 4:1–4; KJV). Paul does not mention an end-times revival but instead a spiritual falling away marked by self-indulgence. Paul notes this explicitly in his letter to the Thessalonians. Here he states, "Now we beseech you, brethren, by the coming of our Lord Jesus Christ, and *by* our gathering together unto him, That ye be not soon shaken in mind, or be troubled, neither by spirit, nor by word, nor by letter as from us, as that the day of Christ is at hand. Let no man deceive you by any means: for *that day shall not come*, except there come a falling away first, and that man of sin be revealed, the son of perdition; Who opposeth and exalteth himself above all that is called God, or that is worshipped; so that he as God sitteth in the temple of God, shewing himself that he is God" (2 Thess 2:1–4; KJV). In another text Paul also makes it clear that people will not be able to come to the truth because of their lawlessness and dullness of spirit. Once again, Paul says to Timothy, "This know also, that in the last days perilous times shall come. For men shall be lovers of their own selves, covetous, boasters, proud, blasphemers, disobedient to parents, unthankful, unholy, Without natural affection, trucebreakers, false accusers, incontinent, fierce, despisers of those that are good, Traitors, heady, highminded, lovers of pleasures more than lovers of God; Having a form of godliness, but denying the power thereof: from such turn away. For of this sort are they which creep into houses, and lead captive silly women laden with sins, led away with divers lusts, Ever learning, and never able to come to the knowledge of the truth" (2 Tim 3:1–7; KJV). Paul nowhere to my knowledge mentions a great final outpouring but rather only a period of lawlessness, hubris, and complete rejection of the things of God. This certainly sounds like what America is witnessing today.

When Peter spoke to the churches in Asia Minor, he, too, warned of coming chaos in the last days. He says, "Knowing this first, that there shall come in the last days scoffers, walking after their own lusts, And saying, Where is the promise of his coming? For since the fathers fell asleep, all things continue as *they were* from the beginning of the creation. For this they willingly are ignorant of, that by the word of God the heavens were of old, and the earth standing out of the water and in the water: Whereby the world that then was, being overflowed with water, perished (2 Peter 3:3–6; KJV). Like Jesus, Peter returns to the days of Noah and describes a period of unbelief, careless ease, and wantonness as opposed to a period of revival and a return to the things of God.

I think Peter's words have a fitting message for the Church today when it comes to the timing of the end-time revival; if there is or was one. He says in 2 Peter 3:8 that a day is like a thousand years and a thousand years are like a day to God. Is it possible that the revival everyone is expecting in the final "days" has already happened with the earlier successive Great Awakenings and we are now experiencing the falling away spoken of by Paul and the "days of Noah" as spoken of by Jesus and Peter? The promise of Joel, which was fulfilled in Acts 2, that God would pour out His Spirit upon all flesh took place in the first century and was renewed at the beginning of the twentieth century at Azusa Street, California, and during similar outpourings of that period. Could it be that the revivals of the past century were all part of the much-anticipated end-time revival? While America has experienced several great moves of the Spirit in various regions over the past hundred years since the Azusa Street revival (the Charismatic Renewal, The Asbury College Revival, Brownsville, etc.), based upon the words of these NT figures, not the least of which is Jesus himself, I am not convinced that there will be a coming great awakening on par with former Great Awakenings. Instead, I am sensing that the Second Coming of Jesus will catch most unawares.

Conclusion

The purpose of this chapter was not to end this book on a downer or to cause people to lose faith in their God. On the contrary, the purpose of this chapter was to offer an honest assessment of what America is facing in the midst of the current chaos. As I reread the words of

Jesus, Paul, and Peter I realized that what they prophesied about the end times certainly reflects the America (and the world) in which I am currently living. We have a culture, and a Church in many cases, that has rejected God; they are scoffers and lovers of themselves; they walk after their own lusts; they have rejected sound doctrine; they have exchanged the truth for a lie; they have hired teachers and pastors who will teach what the people want to hear as opposed to what God actually says. With a Church and culture in such disarray we certainly could use a revival. But alas, people would have to be convinced that they need a Savior. Instead, they have come to the place that in their pride they think they are their own saviors as they embrace "wokeness" and "social justice" and dispense it upon the rest of America for our "own good," or so they believe. Add to this the mantra "trust the science" and you have the perfect blending of hubris and science as their religion. The combination of these elements amounts to a false religion and Christians must take a stand and push back against the Left's religion of wokeness. Like Martin Luther of the Reformation era, it is going to cost the true follower of Christ to stand against tyranny.[153] What I see is not a coming revival—a calm in the eye of the storm of sorts—but rather a coming period of persecution which will refine the Church and make clear for all to see who the true followers of Christ are. The truth is that as a nation and as the Church we are not about to experience the calm before the storm but rather we have sailed our proverbial ship into the center of a "perfect storm."

13

Conclusion: The Perfect Storm

A perfect storm arises when just the right set of circumstances come together to wreak havoc. The 2000 film, *The Perfect Storm*, starring George Clooney and Mark Wahlberg illustrated the phenomenon. This was a heart-wrenching tale of the real-life events about the loss of the Andrea Gail and all those sailing aboard her in a perfect storm on the North Atlantic in October of 1991. While this was a real storm which took place in the past, what America is facing is nothing less than a metaphorical "perfect storm" with a confluence of political, religious, judicial, economic, medical, and cultural elements bearing down on our nation. The gathering storm which we have been speaking about throughout this book is not just any regular storm that will pass with minimal destruction and loss. On the contrary, what we have shown is that the numerous sins along with America's political, judicial, economic, medical, and cultural trajectory is leading us into the perfect storm which will end in the same way the movie about the Andrea Gail ended: in complete disaster and loss.

Those who follow the news will probably recall or be familiar with many of the various political and cultural examples we have discussed or touched on in the preceding chapters. What we have attempted to do is draw together these many examples to highlight the precarious position we are in as a country and to show just how fast we are heading towards the judgment of God. In the same way Ezekiel served as a watchman to warn the people of Judah of coming judgment (3:17–21; 33:1–16), so, too, this book is our attempt to warn churches and the general populace of America by sounding the proverbial trumpet as Ezekiel did in his day. The Enemy has attacked every vital area of our country and culture. He has used the radical Left and the Democrat party coupled with the Deep State, along with "liberal" Christians to set the stage for the gathering storm which has now developed into a perfect storm.

The Dangers of the Left

The central focus of the Enemy has always been the destruction of God's people and everything that is good and wholesome, especially those laws and cultural practices rooted in our Judeo-Christian heritage. Having been founded upon Judeo-Christian principles, and having done much to spread the Gospel of Christ throughout the nations, traditional America, and the American church in particular, are a thorn in the Enemy's side that must be destroyed.

You may be saying that this could never happen in a free country like America. If you are thinking this, I offer a word of warning, this is the path down which every Marxist take over travels. They target the churches and Christians. Allow me to offer an example from recent history. In the introduction to his book *Dark Agenda*, David Horowitz points out the atrocities of the atheistic movements of the 20th century, one of the more disturbing ones being the Marxist communist revolution in Russia. Marxist revolutionaries were responsible for burning 100,000 churches and killing 95,000 of 130,000 imprisoned Russian Orthodox pastors from 1917–1935.[154] Again, some may think this would never happen in America, and again I would offer a word of caution. As a former Canadian I am currently watching my once-great nation, which boasted its religious freedom, turn on Christians and burn and vandalize churches across the country all in the name of wokeness. Pastors who refuse to follow draconian governmental mandates that demand that churches close for the "good and safety" of the masses are being arrested and thrown in jail while liberal Christians hail the government dictates and actions. Supposed "justice" for atrocities and sins of past generations is being exacted from the current generation by social justice "warriors." Horowitz continues by noting that the same ideology, namely, atheistic and anti-Christian stances, resides in the orthodoxy of the American Left. He says, "Radicals in America today don't have the political power to execute religious people and destroy their houses of worship. Yet they openly declare their desire to obliterate religion. In their own minds, their intentions are noble—they want to save the human race from the social injustice and oppression that religion allegedly inflicts on humanity."[55] The key point that Horowitz leaves implicit as opposed to explicit is the reality that the radical Left in America does not have the power to execute religious people and burn their houses of worship *yet*. Make no mistake, this may sound farfetched for America but those who think that this could never happen fail to consider the wickedness of the heart and the depravity of humanity. As I just noted, in Canada, radicals are already burning down churches. Remember that no one thought that the refined and rationalistic French would go on a rampage and murder Christians and anyone who would not bow down to the altar of Reason during the French Revolution. Yet it happened. We are on the precipice of great chaos unless God intervenes. It is all building to the perfect storm.

Americans, and the Church, have stood by and allowed the radicals to take control of our institutions—what is often humorously captured by the phrase, "the inmates have taken over the asylum." But this is no joke. The Left has done its job well. It has now divided America according to class, race, sexual orientation, gender, religious positions, political leanings, and any other "identity" that suits the Left when forming their coalitions for winning elections in order to change laws befitting the Enemy's desire to destroy America. But this is only the opening salvo of why the Left divides us as Americans. They want us at war with each other so they can sweep in and "save the day" with their brand of justice, both social and political. The Church, instead of being countercultural and pushing back against this agenda and repudiating it, have fallen into the trap of wanting to be accepted by the wider popular culture of America. They do not want to be perceived as being whatever "phobe" (homophobe, transphobe, Islamophobe etc.) with which the Left labels their enemies. We have stood by and allowed the Left and those in the Democrat party (including the RINOs) to divide us in the same way the north and the south were divided in the 19th century, which we all know led to the Civil War.

Division is the plan of the Enemy. The progressives have brought back segregation in a most heinous form. They are doing it first and foremost in our institutions of education. Universities were the first of the power structures to fall to the Left. They are now championing segregated dorms and segregated graduations based on race. They mandate safe spaces to "protect" students from "harmful" speech, which is code for any speech the Left deems offensive, namely, conservative or God-centered religious speech. They now are insisting on instituting special days and celebrations for select groups (e.g., African Americans only) where the "oppressive" groups are forbidden to attend thus furthering the divisions. They have invented worthless degrees rooted in identity politics specifically, gender, racial, and ethnic studies that do nothing more than polarize groups and indoctrinate our college-age students that America is bad, Judeo-Christian principles are hateful and bigoted, and that the genders are in a competition and struggle for ultimate power and control.[156] Where will this lead? It is obvious. The Left is dividing us in order to conquer us. Jesus warned us that a nation divided against itself will not stand, yet here we are as a nation regressing to the 19th century. What is our response? We do nothing. Instead, we continue to pay high-priced universities to indoctrinate our children with this drivel and caustic curriculum. We continue to send our minor children to schools that arrogantly tell us that they will continue to indoctrinate our children with CRT, BLM propaganda, perverse sex-ed programs, and false history despite what conservative state legislatures mandate. And we vote politicians into power who openly declare to us that parents have no say in what the state-run schools teach their children. They are doing everything in their power to undermine what America was founded upon: *e pluribus unum* (out of many, one). The perfect storm is upon us.

We are Perverse at Every Level

Isaiah made it clear prior to Judah's exile and destruction that the nation was sick from its head to its toe (Isa 1:1–8). They had rejected their God, and so God brought an indictment against them: they would be desolated by their enemies. Like Judah of the eighth to sixth centuries, America is sick from its head to its toe. We have allowed evil to replace good and we have elevated wicked behavior as normal and acceptable. I do not need to speak in generalities because the specific evidence is available for anyone who wants to see it. There is no more shame about the heinous act of abortion as radicals post videos on social media announcing their joy about killing their unborn babies. They confront abortion protesters outside abortion clinics with a demon-like zeal as they trumpet the killing of their babies. And even in conservative states, radicals go out of their way to rub the blight of abortion in the faces of those who reject this wickedness. No longer is abortion simply an issue of a "woman's right to choose," it is now declared to be sanctioned by God. Recently I (Brian) read a news report describing how abortion activists climbed the Christ of the Ozarks statue in Eureka Springs, Arkansas, and draped a fifty-foot banner over the outstretched arms of Jesus which read, "God Bless Abortions."[157] Such vile wickedness will not go unpunished by God even if we as a nation continue to sanction such acts by legislative actions. And once the Texas heart-beat bill cleared the scrutiny of SCOTUS, the Democrats went apoplectic. Satanists chimed in and declared that abortion is their form of child sacrifice.[158] The vile reality is that the Democrats are now on the same side as the Satanists as defenders of abortion, and some have already noted the praise the Democrats are giving the Satanists for their advocacy! You cannot make this stuff up. The perfect storm is upon us.

We have cities in America canceling 4th of July parades but are more than willing to go ahead and have Juneteenth and gay-pride parades. While in the former case there certainly is nothing wrong with remembering our past, it does become an issue when it is used to divide our nation even more. July 4th parades unite all of us whereas the latter two pander to select portions of our population thus further segregating us. And the central principles motivating gay-pride parades are a direct affront to God's Word and its teaching on proper sexual ethics. When we elevate sexual promiscuity and perversity while rejecting the founding principles of our nation and the Judeo-Christian ideals upon which it was founded, we can be assured that the perfect storm is now upon us.

In Washington, DC, we now have a "president" who pushes through funding for sex changes for US soldiers while many of our veterans are going without basic necessities and care with many living on the streets. The promotion, sanctioning, and funding of perversion with taxpayer dollars is now the rule of the day at the highest levels. The perfect storm is upon us.

At the populace level, the sexual perversion of our nation is reaching new heights. The Left does not just want adults to engage in every form of sexual perversion as "normal" but for some time now they have been eyeing our children to further their perverse ideologies. In July of 2021, the news reported that the Chicago Public School system is now going to mandate that free condoms be made available to children as young as 10 and 11.[159] The depravity of the Left knows no bounds and like the San Francisco Gay Men's Choir announced, they are "coming for our children." The absurdity and obvious purpose of the policy in Chicago is clear. Those enacting it suggest that children at this age can make decisions on whether or not to be sexually active. It is clear that this is another effort not only to sexualize our children, but to make them available to predators as they seek to lower the age of consent. The perfect storm is upon us.

We are Being Programmed

As we have noted, sexual degradation and abortion are not the only issues we are being programmed to accept at all levels of society. We are now passively accepting the fact that we are losing our freedoms. Big Tech is censoring dissenting voices, yet we refuse to walk away from the platforms that abuse us and our free speech. Christians are being targeted for their beliefs by the Left, which now controls most levels of government, local and federal, yet many still walk into the polls on election day and pull the lever for the leftists and their agenda. The perfect storm is upon us.

The medical experts are telling us what we can and cannot do with our bodies, which of course does not apply when it comes to abortion and sex change issues (the hypocrisy is certainly not lost on me), but we sit idly by and allow them to propagate the lies without showing us the hard scientific data proving their unfounded concerns. Instead, we are injecting questionable "vaccines" into our bodies to relieve our fears. The perfect storm is upon us.

We are being programmed to accept in silence the blatant and rampant fraud in our elections, so we will not be labeled a conspiracy theorist or get kicked off our social media platforms. In this vein, we have a justice system that is weaponized against its opponents on the Right, but the MSM and general populace accept it as normal. Thus, we have accepted a two-tiered justice system that harshly prosecutes the average person, or political opponents while allowing the highest level of the political class and those on the Left to get off with the most troubling forms of corruption, violence, and rioting. The perfect storm is upon us.

Over the past two years we have witnessed the reality that most churches are spiritually impotent. It is now clear that many pastors refuse to preach on sin or the Bible, yet we seem to be fine with the status quo because no one wants to rock the boat. Parishioners stay put in dead churches that teach their children nothing more than a social gospel instead of protesting by finding more suitable churches for themselves and their young children. The perfect storm is upon us.

We are watching the Marxist takeover of our nation and the indoctrination of our children with little to no pushback simply because we have believed the MSM and the Left's lies that "Orange man is bad." When God sends people to help us in the midst of the chaos, we either turn a blind eye or reject His help. Can you imagine if the Jews had said in 539 BC that they were not going to accept Cyrus's help to return to their homeland because he was a pagan and a polygamist? We are being programmed to accept the very thing that will be our undoing. The Left, at the behest of the Enemy, is feeding us garbage and evil for a diet and we are so programmed not to fight back that now we accept it willingly as the way things have always been or at least the way they must be now. The perfect storm is upon us.

When I think back to the founding of this nation and the chaos of both the Revolutionary and Civil wars, I am glad we did not have the sheep-like people that occupy our political and religious leadership today. I am glad we had patriots who stood on the Word of God and fought for what was right. Sadly, we are in a state of chaos, confusion, and weakness today because of the decades of programming perpetrated against us by the Enemy of our souls. Because of this, the perfect storm is upon us. The one question that remains is "Is there any hope?"

Our Response

I have said this numerous times and have published this perspective before, but it bears repeating. We must have engagement with culture and politics. Many are isolating themselves from political and cultural concerns because we are told by well-meaning pastors and church leaders that we are not to be overly concerned with these things. I am all for being committed to the things of God for this should be our primary concern; however, it is a false dichotomy to say we cannot do both. We can walk and chew gum at the same time as the well-known quip goes. I am reminded of the words of the Chronicler when describing the men of Issachar in 1 Chronicles 12:32. The men from this tribe were men who had understanding of the times and knew what Israel should do in particular situations. Will this type of response slow or stave off the coming judgment of America? If the Bible has any bearing on this, I would say a heartfelt, yes! I think we can buy some reprieve but mark my words well, judgment is coming! Whether we have another Josiah moment in God's longsuffering mercy remains to be seen.

We also need to be informed Christians. The time for sticking our proverbial heads in the sand is over if we want to save what is left of our country. Many believers do not want to get involved with the political because they insist it is "defiling" to their Christian purity. But knowing one's enemy is important. Moses and Joshua sent spies into the land to reconnoiter their enemy even though God had said he would give them victory. It is the responsibility of pastors, teachers, and church leaders to speak out on political issues that are vital to our existence because of our influence in a representative republic.

We need to take a good long hard look at our children and ask the question of whether that second income is worth throwing them to the leftist "sharks" in the educational system both in K-12 and at university. Homeschooling is still legal and as long as it is, my wife and I will raise our children as the gifts from God that they truly are. Will you? Have you considered sending your child to a private Christian university as opposed to a "free" state school, which is anything but "free" when we lose the souls of our children? We need to remove harmful influences on our children that bombard them on social media, movies, and children's entertainment and instead offer them wholesome alternatives.

There is so much we could do as Americans and as Christians, but I think we may already be too late because, as I noted above, we are already programmed to accept the status quo. We are the frog in the proverbial pot and the water has already reached the boiling point. The gathering storm is here, and it is now at the point of becoming the perfect storm. What will you do to thwart the coming disaster? What will you do to prepare for the devastation that is about to break forth on America in this gathering storm? What will you say to Jesus when he asks you someday the questions: Why did you not act? Why did you not protect your children and instruct them in my ways? So, I ask again, what will YOU do now that the perfect storm is upon us?

Endnotes

1.	^	https://www.thegatewaypundit.com/2021/06/exclusive-accurate-list-2020-election-fraud-cases-shows-87-total-cases-trump-gop-won-71-cases-merits-heard/.

2.	^ See https://www.youtube.com/watch?v=pBP-Lndnkoc.

3.	^	https://weather.com/science/weather-explainers/news/noreaster-snow-rain-wind-northeast-explainer.

4.	^ David Horowitz, David Horowitz, *Dark Agenda: The War to Destroy Christian America* (West Palm Beach, FL: Humanix Books, 2018), 160.

5.	^ See Lance Wallnau, *God's Chaos Candidate* (2016) and *God's Chaos Code* (2020).

6.	^ See https://www.youtube.com/watch?v=PqqIhZeDiWc at 4:53 and 7:40 mark.

7.	^ https://www.youtube.com/watch?v=PqqIhZeDiWc at 8:25.

8.	^	https://www.thegatewaypundit.com/2021/08/conspiracy-theory-aborted-babies-organ-harvesting-leads-true-government-funded/.

9.	^ So, too, Wallnau, *God's Chaos Code*, 69.

10.	^ See a similar conclusion by Wallnau, *God's Chaos Code*, 187–89.

11.	^ Wallnau, *God's Chaos Code*, 187–88.

12.	^ See also the comments of David Horowitz, *Big Agenda: President Trump's Plan to Save America* (Humanix, 2017), 139–44.

13.	^ See discussion by Wallnau, *God's Chaos Code*, 143–45.

14.	^ See Peterson, *What Was the Sin of Sodom, Homosexuality, Inhospitality, or Something Else?* (2016) and *The Bible, Sexuality, and Culture: Raising a Family in a Postmodern and a Post-Christian World* (2021).

15.	^ So, Horowitz, *Dark Agenda*, 93–100.

16.	^	https://www.theepochtimes.com/pro-life-evangelicals-for-biden-feel-used-and-betrayed-open-letter_3724868.html?fbclid=IwAR3ZpSjEeVG3qmjT2Bl9D8TIcmYmWIsb-PERS-VuXMpoEM36fw4BIjYAlaHY.

17. ^ See for example, https://www.westernjournal.com/pro-life-evangelicals-biden-betrayed-man-helped-elect-goes-heads-funds-abortion-covid-relief-package/; https://www.theepochtimes.com/pro-life-evangelicals-for-biden-feel-used-and-betrayed-open-letter_3724868.html; https://churchleaders.com/news/391919-pro-life-evangelicals-who-supported-biden-are-upset.html; https://www.breitbart.com/politics/2021/03/08/nolte-pro-life-evangelicals-for-biden-feign-outrage-over-biden-keeping-abortion-promises/.

18. ^ https://www.washingtonpost.com/politics/2021/04/25/biden-100-days-poll/.

19. ^ https://meaww.com/who-is-deirdre-hairston-catholic-church-calls-cops-on-maskless-pregnant-woman-during-mass.

20. ^ See https://caldronpool.com/christian-leaders-face-six-years-in-prison-for-quoting-the-bible-on-homosexuality/.

21. ^ https://www.thegatewaypundit.com/2021/02/warning-america-four-steps-marxist-takeover-activated-2020/.

22. ^ https://freakonomics.com/2009/08/13/quotes-uncovered-who-said-no-crisis-should-go-to-waste/.

23. ^^ https://citizenfreepress.com/breaking/st-paul-blm-founder-i-resigned-after-i-learned-the-truth/.

24. ^ John M. Ellis, *The Breakdown of Higher Education: How It Happened, the Damage It Does, & What Can Be Done* (New York: Encounter, 2020); Dinesh D'Souza, *Illiberal Education: The Politics of Race and Sex on Campus* (2nd ed. New York: Vintage, 1992); Douglas Murray, *The Madness of Crowds: Gender, Race and Identity* (London, England: Bloomsbury Continuum, 2019).

25. ^ See Ellis, *The Breakdown of Higher Education* (2020).

26. ^ Howowitz, *Big Agenda*, 111.

27. ^ Howowitz, *Big Agenda*, 107–17.

28. ^ https://www.theamericanconservative.com/dreher/political-purge-of-the-armed-forces/; and https://thefederalist.com/2021/01/21/democrats-rally-to-purge-extremists-and-trump-voters-from-national-guard-turning-the-military-into-politics/.

29. ^ https://americanmilitarynews.com/2021/05/heres-the-new-us-army-ad-drawing-controversy-as-woke-or-great-to-see-you-decide/.

30. ^ Elizabeth Bartholet, "Homeschooling: Parent Rights Absolutism vs. Child Rights to Education & Protection," *Arizona Law Review* 62 (2019).

31. ^ https://www.msn.com/en-us/news/world/no-borders-no-walls-no-usa-at-all-eight-arrested-in-denver-during-protests/ar-BB1aJ9Bh.

32. ^ See also comments by David Horowitz, *Blitz: Trump Will Smash the Left and Win* (West Palm Beach, FL: Humanix, 2020), 48–49.

33. ^ Wallnau, *God's Chaos Code*, 64.

34. ^ See Molly Ball, "The Secret History of the Shadow Campaign that

Saved the 2020 Election," *Time* (Feb 4, 2021) at https://time.com/5936036/secret-2020-election-campaign/.

35. ^ https://nworeport.me/2021/05/26/watch-biden-voter-apologizes-to-republicans-says-he-wants-trump-back/.

36. ^ https://www.mymilitia.com/news/view-57-fop-defunding-the-police-results-in-skyrocketing-murder-rates/.

37. ^ https://www.thegatewaypundit.com/2021/07/china-upped-donations-biden-center-400-50m-donations-biden-announced-campaign/.

38. ^ Peachy Keenan, "Bi, Bi, Miss American Pie," *The American Mind* (Mar 1, 2021) at https://americanmind.org/salvo/bi-bi-miss-american-pie/.

39. ^ https://meaww.com/cadbury-creme-egg-ad-with-gay-kiss-triggers-backlash-27000-sign-homophobic-petition-ban-commercial.

40. ^ https://citizenfreepress.com/breaking/san-francisco-gay-mens-choir-we-are-coming-for-your-children/.

41. ^ https://citizenfreepress.com/breaking/milos-take-on-the-san-fran-gay-mens-chorus/.

42. ^ https://theamericansun.com/2021/05/18/fertility-is-a-cultural-thing/.

43. ^ See https://www.americanthinker.com/articles/2021/02/our_supreme_court_goes_full_nicaragua_in_pa_ election_case.html.

44. ^ See for example https://www.facebook.com/106916074935/videos/506916510572301.

45. ^ https://www.jewishvirtuallibrary.org/joseph-goebbels-on-the-quot-big-lie-quot.

46. ^ https://www.washingtontimes.com/news/2020/aug/17/broadcast-coverage-of-trump-95-negative-according-/.

47. ^ See https://www.youtube.com/watch?v=YxLoMkikYiQ.

48. ^ https://www.westernjournal.com/poll-17-biden-voters-abandoned-knew-stories-media-censored/.

49. ^ Zach Vorhies and Kent Heckenlively, *Google Leaks: A Whistleblower's Exposé of Bog Tech Censorship* (New York: Skyhorse, 2021).

50. ^ See https://www.youtube.com/watch?v=YxLoMkikYiQ.

51. ^ Ball, "The Secret History of the Shadow Campaign."

52. ^ Wallnau, *God's Chaos Code*, 124.

53. ^ See especially Horowitz, *Dark Agenda*, 137–58.

54. ^ Horowitz, *Big Agenda*, 71–74.

55. ^ https://thehill.com/opinion/judiciary/561632-rise-of-generation-of-censors-law-schools-latest-battlement-free-speech.

56. ^ https://citizenfreepress.com/breaking/the-nsa-is-spying-on-tucker-carlson/.

57. ^ https://www.thegatewaypundit.com/2021/06/big-brother-biden-administration-wants-americans-report-radicalized-friends-family-government/ and

https://www.thegatewaypundit.com/2021/06/now-audio-proof-fbi-dhs-attempted-recruit-green-beret-infiltrate-oath-keepers-jan-6-riot-recorded/.

58.   ^   https://articles.mercola.com/sites/articles/archive/2021/03/06/milgram-obedience-experi-ment.aspx?ui=56ba98e105921b7f775c5a4092199icc4392bf791f71e0c9272295896ab4d730&sd=20180408&cid_source=dnl&cid_medium=email&cid_content=art1HL&cid=20210306&mid=DM822384&rid=1100396232&fbclid=IwAR3lUsnp-UDrqXpsRIoOAIdDoUfhb7eKygir8aSkHaVaFb19tiJ6GG5fw2m4.

59.   ^ https://www.rt.com/usa/528331-antifa-spa-transgender-exposure-protest/.

60.   ^ https://www.revolver.news/2021/06/five-cases-of-fbi-incitement/.

61.   ^   https://www.thegatewaypundit.com/2021/07/stunning-congressional-first-pelosi-opens-satellite-field-offices-dc-capitol-police-florida-california-deal-regional-threats/.

62.   ^ See Horowitz, *Dark Agenda*, 29–30.

63.   ^ https://citizenfreepress.com/breaking/chinese-mom-chews-out-loudoun-county-you-are-just-like-communist-mao/.

64.   ^ In this regard, I would encourage my reader to check out the important work done by Voddie Baucham. See for example https://www.youtube.com/watch?v=S612gU4UpJM.

65.   ^ See comments by Horowitz, *Dark Agenda*, 30–33.

66.   ^ Horowitz, *Dark Agenda*, 34–35.

67.   ^   https://www.thegatewaypundit.com/2021/07/5000-woke-teachers-sign-pledge-teach-crt-regardless-law/.

68.   ^ https://www.chicagotribune.com/nation-world/ct-aud-nw-union-defend-teachers-critical-race-theory-20210706-26uumdchvng6diaidfl5dxuzgm-story.html and https://www.dailywire.com/news/nations-largest-teachers-union-says-it-will-teach-critical-race-theory-in-all-50-states-1400-school-districts.

69.   ^ Michael Pillsbury, *The Hundred-Year Marathon: China's Secret Strategy to Replace America as the Global Superpower* (New York: St. Martin's Griffin, 2016), 101–14.

70.   ^ Horowitz, *Dark Agenda*, 106–8.

71.   ^ https://www.theblaze.com/news/national-black-power-activist-kill-every-thing-white?utm_content=buffer1b3ac&utm_medium=referral&utm_source=facebook&utm_campaign=fb-glennbeck&fbclid=IwAR1GoWgrdeOmthoAmO-CaDX3wWW6Gujn2-uOtjyLrIQlxRcviODzocIvAvX8.

72.   ^   https://www.thegatewaypundit.com/2021/04/satanic-prayer-hating-white-white-people-included-new-prayer-book-sold-target-video/.

73.   ^   https://www.theblaze.com/news/poll-third-young-adults-proud-to-be-american.

74.   ^ See starting at 44 minutes https://calvarycch.org/i-have-made-

you-a-watchman/?fbclid=IwAR3zoqxUfMGOeCmGkaIvAPj-LmXRgOdi-TS32K_d9jpXQGCxuDK3NtuvrJQ.

75. ^ https://www.commonwealthfund.org/publications/issue-briefs/2020/jan/us-health-care-global-perspective-2019.

76. ^ https://www.realclearpolitics.com/video/2021/04/14/project_veritas_cnn_insider_admits_they_hyped _covid_says_is_gangbusters_for_ratings.html#!.

77. ^ https://www.coffeeandcovid.com/p/what-the-church-needs-to-know-about-covid-19-2307dc2a111c?fbclid=IwAR2uWAlBWNWJ-rDJYOH87Ftlfn-PSDZfpUYloueoBvSmYQowUq_IeOAoUo5I.

78. ^ Hannah Arendt, *The Origins of Totalitarianism* (New York: Harcourt, 1973), 478.

79. ^ https://slate.com/technology/2013/06/sexual-preference-is-wrong-say-sexual-orientation-instead.html.

80. ^ https://childmind.org/article/is-social-media-use-causing-depression/.

81. ^ https://www.psychologytoday.com/intl/blog/the-shameless-psychiatrist/202011/does-social-media-cause-depression.

82. ^ https://www.psychiatrictimes.com/view/covid-19-loneliness.

83. ^ https://www.brainandlife.org/articles/how-loneliness-affects-health/.

84. ^ Cyprian, "On the Mortality," Paragraph 10. Accessed at https://pressbooks.bccampus.ca/ancientandmedieval/chapter/the-plague-of-cyprian-c-252/.

85. ^ https://www.wbur.org/hereandnow/2020/08/24/church-giving-covid-19-pandemic.

86. ^ https://www.anglicansamizdat.net/wordpress/latest-anglican-church-of-canada-membership-and-attendance-statistics/ p.1.

87. ^ https://pulpitandpen.org/2019/08/26/democrats-officially-vote-to-become-party-of-the-non-religious/.

88. ^ https://pulpitandpen.org/2019/08/26/democrats-officially-vote-to-become-party-of-the-non-religious/.

89. ^ https://www.bustle.com/articles/172013-did-democrats-really-boo-god-at-the-dnc-convention-in-2012-controversy-surrounded-this-platform-plank.

90. ^ See the lengthy list of Obama's anti-God actions in Horowitz, *Dark Agenda*, 148–52.

91. ^ See https://www.independent.co.uk/news/world/americas/us-politics/gop-congressman-gender-equality-act-b1807741.html and https://www.thegatewaypundit.com/2021/02/gods-will-no-concern-congress-top-democrat-nadler-derides-god-video/.

92. ^ See Horowitz, *Dark Agenda*, 49–58, 63–74.

93. ^ See the detailed assessment of this by Horowitz, *Big Agenda*, 55–74, 132–34.

94. ^ See also the excellent summary by Horowitz, *Dark Agenda*, 58–61.

95. ^ Peterson, *The Bible, Sexuality, and Culture*, 189–90.

96. ^ https://www.wordhippo.com/what-is/the-meaning-of/arabic-word-d279b2a9caf57e20ec834b335d20c57f9ac44601.html.

97. ^ See https://pjmedia.com/blog/walid-shoebat-and-ben-barrack/2012/02/18/muruna-violating-sharia-to-fool-the-west-n10295.

98. ^ See https://www.dailymail.co.uk/femail/article-9648477/Author-visited-Muslim-mosques-Britain-reveals-no-areas-white-men.html and https://www.thesun.co.uk/news/10669341/muslim-population-england-smashes-three-million-mark-for-first-time/.

99. ^ https://www.lindasarsour.com/bio.

100. ^ https://nycreligion.info/muslims-nyc-area/.

101. ^ https://www.thegatewaypundit.com/2021/06/one-nation-allah-virginia-high-school-graduation-speech-led-islamic-activists-remember-jihad-video/.

102. ^ See http://ijesd.org/papers/26-D435.pdf.

103. ^ https://www.gordonconwell.edu/blog/how-many-muslims-are-there-in-the-united-states/.

104. ^ https://www.theblaze.com/news/texas-judge-due-process-islamic-sharia-tribunal.

105. ^ See Ayaan Hirsi Ali, *Infidel* (New York: Atria, 2007), 268–69.

106. ^ Ayaan Hirsi Ali, *Prey: Immigration, Islam, and the Erosion of Women's Rights* (New York: Harper, 2021), 185–90 esp. 185.

107. ^ In support of this statement, I would direct my reader to the writings of former Islamists, Ayaan Hirsi Ali and Yasmine Mohammed. These two women paint a very ominous picture for the West in light of the rise of Islam.

108. ^ Horowitz, *Big Agenda: President Trump's Plan to Save America* (2017).

109. ^ Horowitz, *Big Agenda*, 27–30.

110. ^ Wallnau, *God's Chaos Code*, 127–28.

111. ^ See my discussion in *The Bible, Sexuality, and Culture*, 15–33.

112. ^ John Adams, "Letter to Officers of the First Brigade of the Third Division of the Militia of Massachusetts, October 11, 1798," in vol. 9 of *The Works of John Adams, Second President of the United States*, ed. Charles Francis Adams (USA: Franklin Classics, 2018), 229.

113. ^ Phyllis Goldstein, *A Convenient Hatred: The History of Antisemitism* (Brookline, MA: Facing History and Ourselves, 2012).

114. ^ See Wallnau, *God's Chaos Candidate*, 26–27.

115. ^ https://www.washingtontimes.com/news/2016/jul/12/obama-admin-sent-taxpayer-money-oust-netanyahu/.

116. ^ Horowitz, *Blitz*, 172.

117. ^ https://www.timesofisrael.com/un-condemned-israel-17-times-in-2020-versus-6-times-for-rest-of-world-combined/. See also Horowitz, *Big Agenda*, 67–68.

118. ^ Horowitz, *Blitz*, 171.

119. ^ https://citizenfreepress.com/breaking/jon-voight-you-liberal-fools/.

120.   ^ https://freebeacon.com/national-security/house-dems-reject-measure-to-boost-israeli-security-aid/.

121.   ^ https://freebeacon.com/national-security/house-democrats-vote-against-hamas-sanctions/.

122.   ^ See also Horowitz, *Big Agenda*, 8.

123.   ^ See the disturbing comments noted by Horowitz, *Blitz*, 90–102.

124.   ^ https://www.newsweek.com/rashida-tlaib-holocaust-anti-semitism-palestinians-republicans-criticism-1423445.

125.   ^ https://minnesota.cbslocal.com/2019/02/11/ilhan-omar-twitter-anti-semitism-aipac-its-all-about-the-benjamins/.

126.   ^ https://citizenfreepress.com/breaking/i-guarantee-trump-won-minnesota/ (start at 12 the minute mark).

127.   ^ See the article by Liel Leibovitz in *Tablet Magazine* titled, "Ignore It at Your Peril: Just Because Trump Said It Doesn't Mean It's Not True: The Democrat Party Is Becoming Unsalvageable." This as noted by Horowitz, *Blitz*, 101.

128.   ^ See http://www.ruthfullyyours.com/2019/08/23/ignore-it-at-your-peril-just-because-trump-said-it-doesnt-mean-its-not-true-the-democratic-party-is-becoming-unsalvageable-by-liel-leibovitz/.

129.   ^ https://nypost.com/2021/05/21/black-lives-matters-obscene-support-for-hamas-terrorism/.

130.   ^ https://www.usatoday.com/story/news/factcheck/2021/05/23/fact-check-black-lives-matter-supports-palestinians-not-hamas/5206977001/.

131.   ^ https://www.thegatewaypundit.com/2021/05/anti-semitic-attacks-increase-across-country-thousands-red-green-allies-gather-washington-dc-national-march-palestine/.

132.   ^ See https://www.facebook.com/leslie.johnson.395891/posts/4418495034845980.

133.   ^ https://rumble.com/vhp8e1-massive-world-renowned-doctor-blows-lid-off-of-covid-vaccine.html.

134.   ^ JesusisComingBack@GoodShepherd316.

135.   ^ The Ingraham Angle https://www.youtube.com/watch?v=lJnPfhD-yow beginning at the 8:32 mark.

136.   ^ https://www.thegatewaypundit.com/2021/07/currently-least-80-central-banks-around-world-looking-digital-currencies/.

137.   ^ https://cryptotapas.com/microsofts-patent-666/.

138.   ^ So, too, Wallnau, *God's Chaos Code*, 103–4.

139.   ^ https://www.thegatewaypundit.com/2021/07/biden-need-go-door-door-literally-knocking-doors-get-people-vaccinated-video/.

140.   ^ https://www.thegatewaypundit.com/2021/07/psaki-will-going-door-door-americans-not-vaccinated-video/.

141.   ^ https://www.thegatewaypundit.com/2021/03/unreal-pregnant-catholic-woman-arrested-holy-mass-not-wearing-mask-ratted-pastor-video/.

142.   ^   https://www.thegatewaypundit.com/2021/03/evil-nike-release-shoe-dedicated-satan-pentagon-human-blood-limited-edition-666-pairs/.

143.   ^ https://uproxx.com/music/lil-nas-x-snl-god-lap-dance/.

144.   ^ Joseph Daniel Unwin, *Sex and Culture* (Oxford: Oxford University Press, 1934) electronic archive https://archive.org/details/b20442580/page/n7.

145.   ^ I have rounded off the date of the sexual revolution to 1960 even though some put it at 1963 or 1968. See https://unherd.com/2021/07/the-wests-cultural-revolution-is-over/.

146.   ^ https://www.youtube.com/watch?v=YtoU4Vb83ZU.

147.   ^ https://www.forbes.com/sites/johnmauldin/2019/11/12/chinas-grand-plan-to-take-over-the-world/?sh=10390c45ab5d.

148.   ^ Pillsbury, *The Hundred-Year Marathon*, 29–30.

149.   ^ Pillsbury, *The Hundred-Year Marathon*, 134–55.

150.   ^ Wallnau, *God's Chaos Code*, 125.

151.   ^ Wallnau, *God's Chaos Code*, 125–26.

152.   ^ Wallnau, *God's Chaos Code*, 154.

153.   ^ Wallnau, *God's Chaos Code*, 128–30.

154.   ^ Horowitz, *Dark Agenda*, 4.

155.   ^ Horowitz, *Dark Agenda*, 4.

156.   ^ See Horowitz, *Big Agenda*, 49–53.

157.   ^ https://citizenfreepress.com/breaking/stay-classy-babykillers/.

158.   ^   https://www.alternet.org/2021/09/satanic-temple/; https://www.thegate-waypundit.com/2021/09/satanists-admit-making-child-sacrifice-abortion-official-ritual-satanic-temple/; https://nypost.com/2021/09/05/satanic-temple-joins-backlash-against-texas-abortion-law/;   https://www.bizpacreview.com/2021/09/05/fittingly-liberals-see-satanic-temple-as-last-best-hope-to-save-abortion-rights-in-texas-1129855/.

159.   ^ https://www.thegatewaypundit.com/2021/07/wth-chicago-public-schools-make-mandatory-provide-free-condoms-5th-graders/.